The Malvinas Question

Uriel Erlich

London
Spanish, **P**ortuguese and **L**atin **A**merican **S**tudies in the **H**umanities

The Malvinas Question by Uriel Erlich

ISBN 9781912399239

Cover image: Grandfather-clock pendulum, *circa* 1833

> "It is crucial that the pendulum movement be brought to a halt [...] when, indeed, the Malvinas Question is no longer a question."
>
> Uriel Erlich

To Natalia, to Mayra,
with love.

Contents

Acknowledgments

This text has its origin in my thesis for the Master of Arts in Public Policy and Development Management at the National University of San Martín (Argentina) and Georgetown University (United States), *The turn in foreign policy in the Malvinas Question from the year 2003: new diagnoses and positioning*. From there, I continued my research.

I want to thank the authorities on the Malvinas Question whom I have interviewed: Andrés Cisneros, Eduardo Airaldi, Fernando Maurette, Fernando Petrella, Javier Figueroa and Jorge Taiana, policy-makers and foreign affairs specialists directly involved in these matters. Their contributions have given the text greater richness. I thank them wholeheartedly for their time and suggestions and for sharing perspectives and experiences, both personal and historical.

Also, to the descendants of Islanders: Alejandro Betts, Cynthia Dickie, Michael O'Byrne, Georgina Gleadell and Guillermo Clifton. I learned about their experiences from a meeting in the Patagonian Observatory on the Malvinas Question, in the city of Río Gallegos, Province of Santa Cruz and, with some of them, I have met and interviewed on more than one occasion. I am grateful to them for sharing their personal and family stories.

I would like most deeply to thank Natalia Parrondo, for her love and recommendations, and for accompanying me in those countless moments in which I sat down to write.

The first edition of this now much revised book, published in Spanish in 2015, was the result of many hours of work as well as the support of those who accompanied me on the journey: Ana Perciavalle, Leandro Gamallo, Marcelo Vernet, Ana Pastorino, María Fernanda Cañas, Inés Tenewicky, Emanuel Damoni, my parents Monica Meschbein and Ruben Erlich, and my sister, Yamila Erlich. The first Spanish edition was prompted by Daniel Filmus, whom I thank for his ongoing trust and support.

This English edition (in which translations from texts originally in Spanish are almost exclusively mine) is a consequence of the support of the University of Nottingham's Department of Spanish, Portuguese and Latin American Studies, and mainly of its Emeritus Professor, Bernard McGuirk, who encouraged me to update my thinking and to publish this new version. I am very grateful for his generosity and recommendations.

Foreword

This book is a valuable contribution to the study of one of the most relevant problems of Argentine foreign policy: the persistence of a colonial enclave in a part of its territory, the Malvinas Islands, usurped by the British since 3 January 1833. As such, it is an enclave that affects the territorial integrity of the country, and the region as a whole; and it is one of the seventeen colonial territories (Non-Self-Governing Territories) recognized by the United Nations, which remain throughout the world.

Uriel Erlich's work focuses the magnifying glass on the history of the policies conducted by successive Argentine governments. It presents an arresting analysis of the continuities and also of the ruptures that the various actions and official perspectives involved, and examines their repercussions upon the Malvinas Question, especially following Resolution 2065 (XX) of the United Nations General Assembly. In this pronouncement of 1965, the international community for the first time recognized that it was a colonial issue, special and particular because it involved a sovereignty dispute that had to be resolved through negotiations between the two parties, Argentina and the United Kingdom. Erlich rightly proposes this historical milestone as a before and after in the treatment of the Malvinas Question.

These pages contribute historical and bibliographic data to the study of the problem, as well as interviews and life stories, all of which allow us further to understand the course of the dispute. After its independence from Spain, Argentina fully exercised sovereignty over the Falkland Islands, until its violent occupation by the United Kingdom in 1833, an intervention which evicted the representatives of the Argentine government and its settlers, preventing it from later establishing a population stemming from their own nation. The said intervention was never consented to by Argentina and, since then, all its governments have supported the claim for the restitution of the islands. Since the historic resolution of the United Nations in 1965, and in consideration of the bilateral negotiations contemplated therein and thereafter, until well into the 1980s, various alternatives for resolving the dispute have been proposed, details of which are documented in this book.

Throughout the period since the 1965 UN pronouncement, there have been two main perspectives from which the different Argentine governments have started: those which understood that in order to enter into any negotiation it was necessary to address the question of sovereignty from the beginning; and those which considered that a series of understandings could be established in various practical matters (communications, flights, fishing resources, among others) that would contribute to a subsequent negotiation for sovereignty.

Erlich's text, organized in stages, makes a journey in multiple registers through the history of those negotiations between Argentina and the United Kingdom, both those that dealt with sovereignty and with practical matters, explaining the perspective from which the policy-makers started, and the national and international contexts that made possible or conditioned the different positions. The author's focus on that part of our history rests particularly on democratic periods, giving an account of the Argentine commitment to recovering the full exercise of sovereignty from the dialogue and negotiation indicated by the international community under the precepts prevailing since 1965. After reading its pages, the perseverance of a State policy established around a cause of not only national but regional and global scope can be visualized, as reflected in the almost two hundred pronouncements of regional and multilateral forums that have addressed the dispute.

Thus it is reported that, in the period 1966-1982, the efforts were aimed at negotiating sovereignty and agreeing, at the same time, on various issues that would improve the lives of the islanders based on communications with the continent: access to flights from LADE to the islands as well as Yacimientos Petrolíferos Fiscales (YPF, the Argentine oil company) and educational exchanges, among others. Until 1982 the UK had not only recognized the existence of the dispute but also even made proposals for the restitution of the territory. The warlike conflict unleashed by the Argentine dictatorship at that juncture did not modify the legal validity of the dispute; again afterwards, United Nations resolutions continued, year after year, urging the parties to resolve the sovereignty dispute. The following seven years, between 1983 and 1989, was the time it took for the re-establishment of bilateral relations between the United Kingdom and Argentina, which happened after the Madrid Agreements of 1989-1990. Erlich shows that, from then on, the axis of Argentine foreign policy in this matter focused on the search for *rapprochement*, both towards the islanders and towards the United Kingdom. The objective was to create conditions such that, when the moment was right, the exercise of sovereignty could be re-negotiated.

The period between 1989 and 2003 was characterized by the complexity of the controversy based on the British unilateral actions. Just as forty-seven bilateral understandings were signed with the United Kingdom, of which about a third dealt with the Malvinas Islands, these entailed a multiplicity of difficulties, especially those linked to economic interests, such as hydrocarbons and fishing resources.

8

The author highlights the great turn in foreign policy that took place in 2003. If the perspective of the 1990s implied the conviction on the part of the referents of Argentine diplomacy that the discussion on sovereignty would arise at the end of a journey of provisional understandings on various topics of common interest, from 2003 on sovereignty became once again the axis of the relationship. This fact was already stated in the first meeting of President Néstor Kirchner with Tony Blair, in July of that year in London, when he expressed to the British Prime Minister his intention to resume negotiations on the sovereignty of the islands.

Regarding provisional understandings, as the United Kingdom continued to carry out numerous unilateral acts, in breach of Resolution 31/49 of the United Nations General Assembly – which urges the parties to refrain from adopting decisions that entail the introduction of unilateral modifications while the sovereignty dispute is in force – Argentina denounced the understanding on hydrocarbons and stopped participating in the Working Group of the fishing commission, among others.

Between 2003 and 2015, the governments of Néstor Kirchner and Cristina Fernández de Kirchner have intensified persistent efforts through diplomatic channels which earned them the support of multiple international organizations. The UN, the OAS, MERCOSUR, UNASUR (since 2008), CELAC (since 2011), SICA, the Ibero-American Summits, the Summits of South America with the Arab and African countries, the G-77 plus China, the meetings of European and Latin American parliamentarians, among others, They endorsed the Argentine position in their resolutions.

I especially want to highlight this approach in that it privileges a historical perspective on the dispute from the occupation of the Islands in 1833, and enables a different vision of Malvinas – not always known – inasmuch as a considerable part of what is imagined on this subject is linked to the conflict of 1982. Within this approach, the text defines that the political decision peacefully to recover the full exercise of sovereignty over the Islands has guided the foreign policy of successive democratic governments throughout history and was reaffirmed in the reform of the Argentine National Constitution of 1994, in the First Transitory Clause, and in the Declaration of Ushuaia, adopted unanimously by the National Congress in February 2012 and thus ratified as a State policy. In turn, it indicates within these policies the creation of the Parliamentary Observatory on the Malvinas Question of the Chamber of Deputies of the Nation, the creation of the Malvinas Museum and, in December 2013, of

9

the Secretariat of Matters Relating to the Malvinas Islands, South Georgia and South Sandwich and the Surrounding Maritime Spaces in the South Atlantic, all of which crystallizes in the organic structure of the State the importance assigned by Argentina to the defence of its legitimate and indefeasible sovereignty rights in the South Atlantic.

I cannot highlight enough the value of the in-depth interviews conducted with Islanders and descendants of Islanders, an undeniable contribution from which life stories arise through the meanderings of foreign policy, as if they were two ways of narrating the same conflict. Always within the academic genre, Erlich appeals to the sociological interview to fathom very little-known aspects of the lives of different generations of people linked to the Islands.

Another particularly significant contribution are the voices of those official representatives of foreign policy who, in different periods, have been interviewed by the author. High-ranking Argentine officials responsible for conducting diplomacy at each stage, such as the Vice Chancellor and Chancellor between 2003 and 2010, Jorge Taiana, and representatives of the Malvinas Area of the Ministry of Foreign Affairs and Worship since 2005, Eduardo Airaldi and Javier Figueroa; or to two Vice Chancellors of the Ministry of Guido Di Tella, Andrés Cisneros and Fernando Petrella, to publicize different aspects of the 1990s' policies on this issue.

In conclusion, we are facing a book that makes a great contribution, not only for those readers who wish to delve into an unresolved problem in the configuration of our country, which involves our region as a whole, but also for those who, from different places and perspectives, we have to involve in the search for the recovery of the full exercise of Argentine sovereignty of the Malvinas Islands.

Daniel Filmus

Secretary of State for the Malvinas, Antarctic and South Atlantic, Ministry of Foreign Affairs, Argentina

Preface

"War changes everything. The matter is closed." Thus has often been the standard response of United Kingdom spokespersons when invited to discuss, let alone enter dialogue, much less negotiation with, Argentine – or other – would-be interlocutors regarding the issue of sovereignty over the Falklands-Malvinas islands. In sum, the door is hardly open and the mind is ostensibly closed. London – officially – speaks not otherwise. Nonetheless, it is not just in Argentina that interest both in a disputed sovereignty and, more broadly, in the territory both geographic and metaphoric of the "too famous glacial islands", in the classic formulation of Jorge Luis Borges, continues to be manifested.

Even as I write, from a British base if not from a closed perspective, books and articles, academic and journalistic, conferences and workshops, research projects and internet debates proliferate. Perspectives shift, predictably, nearly forty years on from the 1982 conflict in the South Atlantic. Whether on the British side, studies on the quite recently released (including Thatcher) government official, however redacted, documents, books of military memoirs or analyses of the prevailing mentalities of the early 1980s or, in Argentina, perhaps more urgently, publications that seek to go beyond the pleas that have fallen on deaf ears by broaching topics other than, but not excluding, sovereignty, the polemic will not lie down, let alone be put to bed. One thinks of the revelations of the UK-based historians Helen Parr (*Our Boys*, 2018) and Grace Livingstone (*Britain and the Dictatorships of Argentina and Chile*, 2018) who, respectively, have exploited the personal interview and the release of government papers in order to break through and beyond fixed national and even nationalistic thinking on transatlantic relations and potentially fruitful re-negotiations between former adversaries.

A prime and yet corresponding previous example of an ambitious attempt to address multiple contextual issues of Argentina's reliance on world, and specifically United Nations, support for a general politics of decolonization, and of the United Kingdom's blanket opposition to such discussions, was Uriel Erlich's 2015 *Malvinas: soberanía y vida cotidiana*. Here, in an extensively revised and updated version in English, *The Malvinas Question*, specialist and general readers alike will find an initial panoramic summary of fifty years of Argentine positionings that soon gives way to a fresh and broadly overlooked other dimension. For Erlich, the focus is on analyzing Argentine policies in their shifting historical contexts, including revelation of the voices and insights of respective decision-makers in successive administrations.

Inseparably, and originally, he brings into sharp focus the views and indeed lives of descendants of Malvinas-born individuals and their families, thereby, and vitally, re-interrogating from an unusual angle Argentine policies and policy-makers of the last half century.

In 1965, Resolution 2065 of the General Assembly of the United Nations triggered the first bilateral negotiations over the said Islands, South Georgia, South Sandwich and the surrounding maritime areas. Erlich's strategy depends on interviews that allow interested parties to speak for themselves. His study opens the ears of those who, often, might hear but not necessarily listen to preoccupations and ambitions both historically situated and still urgent for all who would aspire to understand why the matter is not closed and only illusorily bracketed out: "None so deaf as those who will not hear", as the old saying goes. Let there be no doubt, the strongly contrasting phases addressed by Erlich's book, basically the 1990s *rapprochement* and the 2003-2015 and current reaffirmations of sovereignty claims and insistence on negotiation, have been and are being heard in London and beyond.

The author, a professional sociologist who has worked in the Malvinas Secretariat of the Ministry of Foreign Affairs of Argentina, has been ideally placed therefore to have had access to both sources and voices pursued during the period of the informed and meticulous research and field-work manifested in the present volume. The echo-chamber of both history and a serious listening to other voices, authentic and expressing no little passion, reminds us of the potential and rarely more urgent need for resistance to ostensible closing of ears and minds... on all sides and all fronts.

Bernard McGuirk

Professor Emeritus of Romance Literatures and Literary Theory,
University of Nottingham

President of the International Consortium
for the Study of Post-Conflict Societies

Author of *Falklands-Malvinas: An Unfinished Business*

Introduction

The year 2015 marked the 50th anniversary of Resolution 2065 (XX) of the United Nations General Assembly, through which the international community recognized the existence of the sovereignty dispute between Argentina and the United Kingdom of Great Britain and Northern Ireland on the Question of the Malvinas Islands. The said pronouncement, dated 1965, also urged both countries to negotiate and established the importance of resolving the controversy by peaceful means. The thorny issue has existed since 1833, after the British occupation of the islands by force. Likewise, the Resolution strengthened Argentina's position in that it called on the United Kingdom to negotiate, which it refused to do.

In January 1834, a year after the British landing on the islands and after seven months of silence at the protest of the then Argentine minister, Manuel Moreno, the British Foreign Secretary, Lord Palmerston, responded that he expected the government of the United Provinces would be satisfied and stop discussing His Majesty's sovereign rights over the islands. "From now on, the password in the Foreign Office was not to respond to Argentine claims, but rather a refusal to restart the discussion" (Groussac, 1982), a stance which was maintained until Resolution 2065 (XX).

The aim of this book is to address the development of Argentine foreign policy on the Malvinas Question since the aforementioned recognition of the United Nations General Assembly, from which point the government of the United Kingdom accepted, for the first time in history, to sit down to negotiate on the sovereignty of the Malvinas Islands. An analysis of the respective and various stages of foreign policies on the Malvinas Question is carried out, dating from the 1965 pronouncement to the present, for the purpose of which we must refer to the origins of the conflict.

The Question of the Malvinas Islands is understood as the sovereignty dispute pertaining between Argentina and the United Kingdom of Great Britain and Northern Ireland over the Malvinas Islas (Falkland Islands), Georgias del Sur (South Georgia), Sandwich del Sur (the South Sandwich Islands) and the surrounding maritime spaces.

Argentina's foreign policy on the Malvinas in the period under analysis can be characterized, broadly, from two perspectives. One states that, while it is not possible to force the United Kingdom to discuss sovereignty, it must cooperate on other issues as a way to start a path that is expected to promote a climate conducive, when the time comes, to addressing the substantive discussion. The other proposes a policy that, although it is not the opposite, starts from a different diagnosis: the discussion of sovereignty should be a central part of the agenda, from the beginning of the negotiations that may be started between both countries. To enhance understanding of each stage of the process, its particularities and contexts, the book will focus on the twists and turns of the adopted policies, their characteristics, the reasons that gave rise to them and their consequences.

Each stage approached was thus guided by a series of questions. In what contexts, international and national, was the Malvinas Question pursued, and what have been their impact on the issue? What have been the characteristics of Argentine foreign policy in which the stances on Malvinas were successively framed? What were the diagnoses and perspectives from which policy-makers started out? How did their diagnoses impact upon the policies that were carried out with respect to the Islands? What have been the consequences of each of the policies implemented?

Chapter I will address the British military occupation of the islands by force in 1833, an action which cut off the legitimate exercise of Argentine sovereignty, rendered effective after its independence from Spain. By way of contextualizing the issue, we shall refer to the history of the colonies, in which France, Spain and Britain had a presence in the archipelago. This path shows the legitimacy of the sovereignty of Spain over the islands, which exercised all the powers of government between 1767 and 1811, a period in which – among other actions – they appointed thirty-two governors of the islands. The legitimacy of Argentine sovereignty is based on the *succession of States*, after their independence from Spain, as the concept is one of the modes of acquisition of territories recognized by International Law. Throughout history – and unlike other colonial enclaves – Argentina never gave up claiming its legitimate sovereign rights over the islands, a position which maintained the legal validity of the controversy.

In Chapter II, the course of Argentine foreign policy will be analyzed, from Resolution 2065 (XX) of the United Nations General Assembly in 1965, to the conflict of 1982. The pronouncement signified the international community's recognition of the existence of the sovereignty dispute and contributed, after more than one hundred and thirty years, to the start of negotiations with the United Kingdom. The stage was marked by the negotiations between Argentina and the United Kingdom over sovereign rights as well as on practical matters, in the context of the decolonization process, which had begun after the end of the Second

World War.

In Chapter III, the military conflict will be analyzed in the context of the last *dictadura cívico-militar* [civic-military dictatorship] of Argentina from the perspective of foreign policy. We shall address the implications of that regime in the history of the dispute, which had developed peacefully since the beginning of the controversy and would continue in this way after the seventy-four-day conflict.

The stage between 1983 and 1989, addressed in Chapter IV, is part of the return to democracy in Argentina under the government of Raul Alfonsín. The period is characterized by the breakdown of relations with the United Kingdom and unsuccessful attempts to re-establish them. Argentina proposed to continue addressing the substantive dispute and the United Kingdom refused to do so. After the war, Argentine diplomacy kept the legal dispute in force after obtaining new pronouncements from the United Nations. Likewise, in this period, began the conversations that allowed, in the following period, for the resumption of relations with the United Kingdom.

The new orientation of considerations concerning the Malvinas Question began at the same time as a profound change in the international context, marked by the fall of the Berlin Wall, and Argentine foreign policy alignment with the United States; the United Kingdom was the latter's strategic ally. The Madrid Agreements of 1989 and 1990 allowed for the re-establishment of relations between Argentina and the United Kingdom, beginning the new stage to be explored in Chapter V, as characterized by its policy-makers. Under the governments of Carlos Menem, the Alliance and Eduardo Duhalde, it was orientated towards *rapprochement* with the United Kingdom and the islanders, mainly through the establishment of a series of provisional understandings on practical matters between the two countries. Likewise, the Argentine legal claim continued and efforts were made to obtain the support of other countries and of international organizations.

Chapter VI will address the Malvinas Question between 2003 and 2015, under the governments of Néstor Kirchner and Cristina Fernández de Kirchner. Starting in 2003, there was a shift in Malvinas policy, in the context of a general realignment of foreign policy, which was reorientated towards the Latin American region. The British unilateral actions showed that if the aim of the provisional understandings was to create a climate conducive to addressing the sovereignty dispute, the United Kingdom had not acted accordingly. The axes that structured this period were the *end of the demalvinization process*, the *firmness in the bilateral relationship* and the *search for external support* in the context of the emergence of new regional organizations and a growing integration of the region.

Finally, a chapter of conclusions is offered, in which the development of the stages is recapitulated, their continuities are reviewed and, by way of closing, an analysis is proposed on the policy orientations that, in our opinion, favour the Argentine position on this important claim of its legitimate sovereignty rights over the Malvinas Islands, a claim which has never been abandoned since 1833. For the present edition, we include a new chapter, "Onwards, 2015...", summarizing and explaining the processes and events that have happened and re-shaped this important international matter since the first publication of this book in 2015.

The research focused on various sources: the survey of official documents on the Malvinas Question, the development of semi-structured interviews with key informants, the systematic registration of the main Argentine periodic press (*Página 12* and *La Nación*, in relation to the Malvinas Question of the last periods), and the survey of documents of international organizations and regional organizations. Interviews were carried out mainly with senior officials of the *Ministerio de Relaciones Exteriores y Culto de la Nacion* (Ministry of Foreign Affairs and Worship) of Argentina, who have been policy-makers on the Malvinas Question. Stories of descendants of islanders are also included in the book. They live in various locations in continental Argentina and their families, at least in part, lived or live on the islands. These stories permit us to understand foreign policy from an alternative perspective.

Malvinas is part of our legacy and our history. Malvinas has been a national cause since it was occupied by force by Great Britain in 1833, and is also a cause of great concern to ex-combatants. It is also a dispute, not only about sovereignty but also about resources. Malvinas is one of the last seventeen Non-Self-Governing Territories (colonial territories) recognized by the United Nations.[1] Ten of them are under British possession.

The Question of the Malvinas Islands has been widely discussed since the beginning of the dispute, and has been analyzed from the time of Paul Groussac, in his book *Les Îles Malouines*,[2] to the present. In recent

---

[1] The seventeen Non-Self-Governing Territories are Anguila, Bermuda, Gibraltar, Guam, the Cayman Islands, the Falkland-Malvinas Islands, the Turks and Caicos Islands, the British Virgin Islands, the United States Virgin Islands, Montserrat, New Caledonia, the Pitcairn Islands, French Polynesia, Western Sahara, Samoa, Saint Helena and Tokelau.

[2] Groussac was director of the National Library of Argentina for 44 years. He

decades it has generated a large number of studies related to the 1982 war, its causes, characteristics and consequences. Among other issues, the most prominent have been the relationship of the Malvinas Islands to the concepts of nation and memory, the civic-military dictatorship and the military conflict, the problems of former combatants and war veterans, the place that the Islands occupied in the social imaginaries of different times. More than thirty years after the war, attentive to its social significance and the tragedy that it was, and above all in consideration of the deaths during the conflict and the numerous suicides of former combatants following it, I intend to address the dispute in extended perspective, recovering the broader history and focusing on Argentine foreign policy. I hope to present unknown aspects of a familiar history that is still in force and in dispute: the Malvinas Question.

---

published *Les Îles Malouines* in 1910. In September 1934, the work was published in Spanish following the sanction of the National Law N° 11.904 with unanimous support, after it was presented by Senator Alfredo Palacios in the Argentine Parliament.

I
The question of the Islas Malvinas: the origin of the conflict

> I am a patriot because *Patria* comes from father. It is the land of my parents, my grandparents.
>
> Marcelo Vernet, great-great-grandson of Luis Vernet, First Argentine Political and Military Commander in the Malvinas Islands

Life in the islands

Alejandro Betts was born in the Islands in 1947, given the name Alexander. For 34 years he had no nationality because the British did not recognize the native islanders. Of a fourth generation born in the islands, he defines himself as *fueguino* (a Fuegian). His Irish great-great-grandfather came to the Islands in 1842. His great-great-grandmother arrived in 1854 from Scotland. It was then a common policy of the United Kingdom to effect the colonization of overseas territories through voyages from the coastal towns of Great Britain and Ireland.

Betts refers to the Islands as "the territory" and as "the colony" interchangeably. It is the territory because it is a geographical space that is built, lived in and apprehended. But it is also the colony because therein can be found the main feature that defines this region, its relationship with the colonial power.

From his years at school, Betts recalls that he wondered: "how is it that Argentines claim to have rights while the British beat us down, saying: 'rest assured, our right is irrevocable, ignore them'?" Faced with such questions, the teachers advised, "Don't get involved in things that don't concern you"; or in the best of cases, they would say to him, "I cannot answer that question. You should consult an official of the colonial administration."

His family, who worked in the fields, named the rural animals in Spanish. "Where does it come from?" Betts asked his uncle. "I have heard that at some point the Spanish were on the islands," the uncle replied. When Betts tried to check with the local government, the answer was always the same: "it does not concern you", "it is irrelevant". As the years passed and he grew into an adult, these denials piqued his growing interest. There must be something they weren't telling him, a missing piece in the puzzle.

Betts took up distance learning, became a qualified accountant through the International Correspondence School (ICS), and got a job in a local supermarket. "With the title under my arm, I thought I was going to have a great future in Puerto Argentino. But they gave me a stall at the West Store, the famous Falkland Islands Company warehouse, as if to say 'conform'." At the same time, in the early 1970s, the only tourism that came to the islands was from the continent. One day, an Argentine tourist told him, "Malvinas are Argentine." Betts replied, "Madam, I'd like to know if your statement is true, but here I don't know how to confirm it." Betts had always assumed that it was impossible to find documentary proof that the Malvinas belonged to Argentina. "I'm going to get you the documentation," the lady answered. "But I'm going to send it to you on the condition that you read it, analyze it, and draw some conclusion consistent with your conscience"

A few months later Betts received the document in the mail. It was a copy of the Dictum of the National Academy of History of Argentina, which explained the legitimate right of Argentina to sovereignty of the Malvinas Islands. "I read it. I left it. I read it again," says Betts. "Still not convinced, I thought: we in the Islands are unaware that there was a French colonization of the territory. Is it true that there were French in the Malvinas? It occurred to me to write to France."

So it was that he sent a note to the consulate in France requesting information, and weeks later he received a copy of the instructions issued by Louis XV, who had appointed Michel François Bougainville de Nerville, a relative of Louis Antoine de Bougainville, as French governor in Malvinas in 1764 on the eastern island, founding Port Louis. The instructions required the incorporation of the Malouines into French overseas possessions. The other document he received was a copy of the Family Treaty, signed between the cousins Louis XV of France and Carlos III of Spain, with its legal recognition of pre-existing Spanish sovereignty, in which the parties agreed to support each other in the event of invasions.

"French colonization was proven," says Betts. "Spain in the Falklands? I had to confirm the Spanish presence, which I suspected was true from my uncle's comment." He wrote to the consulate in Spain. After a few months he received a copy of the list of the thirty-two Spanish governments in the Malvinas that had served with effective royal residence in Puerto Soledad, from 1767 to 1811, from Felipe Ruiz Puente to Pablo Guillén. Everything about the legal basis of the Dictum was beginning to be confirmed. After its independence from Spain was gained, the sovereignty of the islands corresponded, by succession of States, to Argentina.

"I continued investigating," says Betts, "until I realized that there was no misrepresentation of the facts by Argentina. The Malvinas are

Argentine. And if they are Argentine, in my family we have four generations of natives. We were Argentines." This conclusion left him alone. "In my family, the only one who openly accepted and assimilated that position was me." His brothers heard him out but did not accept his conclusions. "It seems to me that the British have led us by the nose down a path that is not correct," Betts explains. "I have evidence that the British came and occupied the islands. It was not a territory without inhabitants as they always told us."

Fundamentals of history[1]
The Malvinas Question refers to the territorial dispute between Argentina and the United Kingdom following British occupation of the islands. In 1965, that dispute was recognized by the international community, which has since urged negotiations between the two parties.

The Spanish had withdrawn from the Malvinas in 1811, simultaneous with Argentine independence. In 1820 the government of Buenos Aires sent a frigate to the islands to take possession and reaffirm its rights. Around 1829 it created the Political and Military Command of the Malvinas Islands and the islands adjacent to Cape Horn in the Atlantic, with Luis Vernet as its commander. On 20 December 1832, Britain began a military operation and at the beginning of 1833 expelled the Argentine authorities who were legitimately there, establishing, from then on, British administration and an immigrant British population.

The Argentine Republic has not since stopped protesting at the illegitimate occupation of the islands. From the beginning of the controversy it has always maintained its legal claim. International law – with its reference to customs, international conventions and recognized general principles – supports this claim. The official Argentine position presents the Malvinas Islands as part of an illegally occupied Argentine territory: an act of force deprived the country of possession of the archipelago, which, as it was never consented to, did not create any right. The British action of 1833 was part of the imperialist policy of the European powers during the nineteenth century in America, Asia and Africa.

The legitimacy of the Argentine position is based on the right derived

---

[1] The fundamentals of the official Argentine position can be traced, among a variety of documents, in the Dictum of the National Academy of History, in the statement of Senator Alfredo Palacios in the Senate of the Nation in 1934, in the statement of Ambassador José María Ruda before the United Nations in 1964, and in the document of the Foreign Ministry, *Argentina's position on various aspects of the question of the Malvinas Islands* (2012).

after Argentine independence was gained from Spain, as one of the modes of "acquisition of territories" recognized in international law: when a colony becomes independent from the colonial power, the nascent sovereign state inherits the territory the colonial power possessed as a colony. France, the first power to occupy the islands, had recognized the Spanish right to them. Argentina, a nascent state, was the legitimate heir to the erstwhile Spanish territory.

Around 1766, international law considered occupation necessary for the acquisition of *res nullius* territories, and not their discovery: in 1592, John Davis, an English navigator, had sighted the islands, but they were not occupied. When the British settled in Port Egmont, in the Falkland Islands, in 1766, 174 years after having first sighted them, it was not an empty territory, subject to appropriation, but had already been occupied by the French and Spanish. The French sailor, Louis Antoine de Bougainville, had founded Port Louis in the East Malvinas in 1764, in the name of the King of France.

> The first effective occupation was that of France in 1764, which recognised the rights of Spain, restoring the settlement to her, whereby the effective Spanish occupation antedates the British presence. The latter continued during the eight years when the English were in Port Egmont and afterwards. (Ruda, 1964)

Two years after the French occupation, in 1766, Britain sent a clandestine expedition that founded Port Egmont, on Saunders Islet, next to the West Malvinas. Bougainville had called it Port de la Croisade. Around 1 April 1767, France completed the delivery of Puerto Luis to Spain, and it was renamed Puerto Soledad. International custom requires countries to express their reservations in the face of events that they do not recognize as legitimate. Britain did not express any reservations, and so Spanish rights were unchallenged.

In 1770, Spain forcibly expelled the British from Saunders Islet and, on this occasion, Britain made a claim before the Court of Madrid. Spain promised to restore things to the *status quo ante*, but made explicit its rights over the islands, which the British accepted:

> A solution was finally arrived at on 22 January 1771. Spain's ambassador to London, Prince de Masserano, declared that his Sovereign "disapproves the aforementioned violent enterprise and binds himself to re-establish matters as they were prior to the episode", adding that "the restoration to His Britannic Majesty of the

21

Port and Fort called called Egmont cannot and must not in any way affect the question of prior sovereign rights over the Malvinas Islands." This declaration was accepted by the Government of His Britannic Majesty on the same day, and under Lord Rochford's signature, it was stated that His Britannic Majesty would consider the declaration of the Prince of Masserano, with the entire fulfillment of the agreement by His Catholic Majesty as adequate redress for the affront done to the Crown of Great Britain. (Ruda, 1964)

From this diplomatic act, the acceptance of the Spanish declaration stands out: Britain did not challenge Spanish sovereignty of the islands.

Britain's silence in the light of such an express, and written, reservation, can only be interpreted in its true form, namely, as an acceptance which, furthermore, is borne out by the original title of the British document, which is not called a "Counter-Declaration", as Lord Palmerston called it in 1834, but "Acceptance", according to the Official Edition of the State Papers of 1771. (Ruda, 1964)

All British documentation refers to the return of Port Egmont to *status quo ante*, but not to the Malvinas Islands in general.

As stated by the Argentine Ambassador José María Ruda at the United Nations in 1964 – and later confirmed by UN Resolution 2065 (XX) the following year – the British occupation was illegal. It violated current treaties. It was clandestine. It was concealed until the Spanish managed to verify it. It was late. It happened after the French occupation and the accession of Spain. It was answered. Spain put up resistance and the explicit British reservation was partial, since it was reduced to Port Egmont and did not include Puerto Soledad or the entire archipelago, then Spanish possessions. This British reservation was brief, lasting only eight years, and it was precarious: from 1774 it was abandoned. "Falkland's Island is mentioned in the possessive singular, which, linked to the British acceptance of the fact of the Spanish possession of Puerto Soledad, proves that the English claims were limited – during their stay in Port Egmont – exclusively to this settlement and not to the entire archipelago" (Ruda, 1964).

After the voluntary abandonment of Port Egmont by the British, they made no claim on the islands for almost sixty years. Only then, in a context in which their expansionist zeal resurfaced, did they violently evict the Argentine population from the islands. There is no continuity between their few years of presence in Port Egmont and their landing of

1833. Moreover, there were also international treaties – sources of law – that strengthened Argentina's position. The Treaty of London of 1604 between Spain and England, that of Madrid of 1670 and that of Utrecht of 1713-1715, recognized the rights of Britain in North America, at the same time that they prohibited British shipping in the South Sea and trade in the Spanish Indies.

Spain, from 1767, exercised all the powers of government: in 1776 they created the Viceroyalty of the Río de la Plata, including the islands; in 1777 they destroyed the buildings and constructions of Port Egmont; and they named, between 1767 and 1811, thirty-two Spanish governors. As Ruda (1964) stated, "England's silence over the Malvinas between 1774 and 1829 confirms her recognition of Spanish rights and her desire not to return to the Archipelago."

Towards the end of the eighteenth century, the San Lorenzo Convention of 1790 recognized the British right to establish colonies only on the coast of North America, while in the remainder of the area, Spain admitted only the right to fish. The signatory countries undertook not to establish new colonies in the southern Pacific and Atlantic oceans, thus maintaining the *status quo*. The commitment was not to populate what was already occupied by Spain – Spain had been in the Malvinas since 1767 – and not to sail less than ten leagues from its coasts.

With the beginning of the independence period, Argentina exercised all the powers of government:

> In 1820, Colonel David Jewett, commander of our frigate *Heroína*, took public and solemn possession, with twenty-one gun salutes, of the archipelago, on behalf of the government of Buenos Aires and in the presence of the famous English navigator James Weddell, who was stopping at the Malvinas during his first Antarctic voyage and recalls this fact in his *Voyage towards the South Pole*, published in 1825. (Palacios, 1934)

In 1820, Jewett notified the English and North American ships that were in the waters of the Malvinas Islands that Argentine laws regulated hunting and fishing there and that transgressors would be sent to Buenos Aires to be tried. There was then no opposition to the assertion of Argentine law in the archipelago, nor did Britain file a claim, even though the facts were published in newspapers in their country, as well as in the United States and other countries.

By then, the Argentine government intended to populate the islands. In 1823, it offered Luis Vernet and his partner, Jorge Pacheco, as compensation for State debts, a concession on the islands for commercial purposes: the exploitation of wild cattle and horses and the usufruct of fishing and hunting amphibians. Vernet, a merchant from Hamburg resident in Buenos Aires since 1817, set out together with his partner to expand the activities he was already developing in the south of the country, towards the islands. Argentina promoted the settlement of the islands from then on.

In February 1824 the first of the expeditions arrived in Malvinas, in which Emilio Vernet (Luis's brother) and his brother-in-law, Loreto Sáez travelled. They settled in Puerto Soledad. Luis Vernet journeys to the Malvinas from 1826.

> Luis Vernet is personally in charge of colonizing the Islands. Applies an orderly and methodical administration of natural and strategic resources that strengthens Argentine sovereignty over the archipelago; it activates new commercial zones and spreads the economic capacity of the islands in national and foreign economic-financial centres. (Vernet, 2011)

The results of their investigations are reported to the government of Buenos Aires. "These reports include news, topographic surveys, scientific explorations and agricultural experiments; and in particular the opportunities and feasibilities to establish a fixed population" (Vernet, 2011).

On one of the trips Luis Vernet made to Buenos Aires, he requested that he be granted ownership of the vacant land on Soledad Island and State Island – on which there was wood – with the commitment to establish a settlement with fixed settlers. The support of the Argentine government was necessary to populate the islands and found new ports for the fishing trade. A Decree of 11 January 1828 granted the request. In turn, the national government ordered that Puerto Soledad be the seat of the Malvinas government.

In less than two years, Puerto Soledad had more than a hundred stable inhabitants. At Vernet's request, he was given 4 cannon and 50 rifles to fortify the island, defend the settlers and the coasts, and enforce the law on the protection of fishing.

The first settlers were rural workers from the Argentine provinces and Uruguay, and as of 1828 the immigration of workers from other countries was encouraged, "which promoted livestock, fishing and hunting of sea lions and seals, salting fish and beef, leather tannery" (Vernet, 2012).

On 10 June 1829, Vernet was appointed First Political and Military

Commander of the Malvinas Islands and adjacent to Cape Horn in the Atlantic Ocean, and settled in Puerto Soledad. His wife, María Sáez de Vernet, had three children when she arrived in the islands on 15 July 1829. Some time later, her fourth child was born in Puerto Soledad, a girl they named Matilde *Malvina* Vernet. María Sáez de Vernet's diary allows us to recover something of the daily life then on the islands. It speaks of the races, frequent in the town, of the dances on Sunday afternoons, and of marriages. It records the weather. It tells of the construction of properties, such as on 20 August 1829, when "the Germans finished their house: Vernet had assigned the one that served as a Hospital to the Spaniards" (Vernet, 2016), with thick stone walls on which, only until that day, doors and windows were missing.

> The expedition was accompanied by 23 families who were going to swell the existing Argentine population. That same day [María Sáez de Vernet] began to write a diary. Nothing extraordinary is referred to in its pages. Just the daily life of a small town where residents of the provinces of Santiago del Estero, Entre Ríos, Córdoba, Buenos Aires and Santa Fe share their luck; countrymen from Uruguay and Tehuelches from deep Patagonia; German peasants, who together with the Argentines build their houses; Scots and French who, forgetting the sea, become horsemen and work alongside our countrymen; Genoese, English, Irish fishermen and sailors. Men who bring their trades as their only fortune. Africans also found a distant home there, who, due to the vicissitudes of the war with Brazil, where they were destined as slaves, ended up being Malvinas settlers. (Vernet, 2012).

On Sunday 30 August 1829, Luis Vernet took possession of the islands on behalf of the government of Buenos Aires. "At twelve o'clock the inhabitants met, the National flag was raised, at which time twenty-one cannon shots were fired, repeating incessantly *¡Viva la Patria!*" (Vernet, 2016). María put a ribbon in the colours of the Argentine flag on each one of them, and the Commander introduced himself.

Towards September, María was looking forward to the arrival of a ship from Buenos Aires, as she wanted news of her family. Ships are a recurring theme in the diary: discovering the ship's flag allowed them to know if it was friendly or potentially hostile. On 12 September, the ship from Buenos Aires arrived, bringing letters sent from the Vernet family. Another ship arrived on 25 September, from which they unloaded supplies of biscuits, flour, honey, brandy, tea, coffee, beans, clothing, gunpowder and ammunition, three large whaling boats, pipes and barrels, cucumber, vinegar, and soap. A new ship appeared on 19 October. Vernet speculated all day, because until dark it had not come close enough. The same thing happened on 1 November: a ship was sighted, which finally arrived with a sick person seeking help.

During these years the expansionist zeal of Britain resurfaced: the archipelago reassumed importance for colonial navigation. Britain then protested at the creation in November 1829 by Argentina of the Political-Military Command of the Malvinas Islands, claiming that it was inconsistent with British rights over them. The United States, for its part, showed interest in protecting the seal-hunt that was carried out from ships flying its flag off the coast of the Islands.

> It was then, in the heyday of the expansionist eagerness of Great Britain, that the English interest in the Archipelago was awakened, an interest that was nothing but the renewal of its old aspirations of possessing land in the South Atlantic. (Ruda, 1964)

Luis Vernet detained three boats in 1831 to enforce Argentine legislation on fishing, when the US corvette Lexington appeared in Puerto Soledad, flying the French flag. US sailors landed on the islands and destroyed an Argentine settlement. The United States wanted the immediate return of one of the detained fishing boats and demanded that the political-military commander of the Malvinas end his intervention in the activities of their ships. This diplomatic incident between Argentina and the United States ended in a virtual rupture of relations between the two countries.

The events that followed this altercation revealed the powerful, mutually supportive relation between the United States' representative in Buenos Aires and the English Chargé d'Affaires.

> [...] the British die was cast: the British Admiralty instructed captain Onslow to set sail for the Malvinas, and on January 3, 1833, the corvette Clio appeared off Puerto Soledad. A small Argentine vessel, the Sarandi was riding at anchor. The English captain insisted that the Argentine detachment withdraw. The difference in numbers allowed of no possible fight and added to that was the element of surprise.
>
> The Argentine leader replied to the order by saying that "he held Great Britain responsible for the outrage and the violation of the respect due to the Republic, and its rights that were being assaulted by force – as blind as it was irresponsible" and added that "he was

withdrawing, but that he refused to lower his flag."

The British thereupon lowered the Argentine flag and by force, occupied Port Soledad. Thus, by plunder, another chapter of colonial history was written. Almost all the Argentine inhabitants of the Islands were then evicted. (Ruda, 1964)

Almost six decades after the voluntary withdrawal of 1774 from Port Egmont, the British committed this act of force in Puerto Soledad, on West Malvinas Island, where they had never been. The following year they occupied the entire archipelago.

The Argentine reaction was immediate. On 15 January 1833 a claim was filed with the English Chargé d'Affaires in Buenos Aires, and a further claim was presented on 22 January. From the beginning of the dispute, the Bolivian government expressed its support for Argentina "to obtain reparation for such an offence". Through an official letter dated 14 June 1833 from its Minister of Foreign Affairs, Dr Mariano Enrique, to Dr Manuel García, Minister of Foreign Affairs of Argentina, it expressed solidarity with the Argentine Republic in the face of the occupation, asserting that it constituted an offence to all the Latin American republics. On 24 April 1833 the Argentine government had presented a protest note to the British government, which it reiterated on 17 June. Britain's response of 8 January 1834, seven months later, claimed British rights to the original discovery and subsequent occupation of the islands, which was again rejected by Argentina on 29 December 1834. Since then, Britain has maintained its position and Argentina has continually repeated its protest.

For 132 years, Britain was reluctant to negotiate sovereignty rights over the islands. It was in 1965, a year after Ambassador Ruda's statement, that the United Nations General Assembly passed Resolution 2065 (XX), which recognized the sovereignty dispute over the Islands between Argentina and Britain, and urged both parties to reach a resolution. The United Kingdom agreed for the first time to enter into negotiations.

II

1965-1982: the negotiations

Get out of isolation

Alejandro Betts's first work experience had been in rural establishments. When he finished primary school in 1961, he began travelling around the islands and working in the fields. He enjoyed that life, but in order to improve himself he decided to continue studying. He married his first wife, Candy, in 1969 at the age of 21, and had two children, Dawn and Paul. After qualifying as an accountant, he worked first in a market for the Falkland Islands Company (FIC) – the islands' monopoly company, which at that time handled most of the commercial activities – and then as Secretary General of the Association of Landowners of the islands. There he kept the accounts for around a dozen farms.

His wife died in 1977. In 1979 he joined the Argentine State Air Lines (LADE), a subsidiary of the Air Force, in the Puerto Argentino office. After competing for the position, he was hired as civilian personnel. A short time later, he received a new proposal from another Argentine company to carry out additional tasks at Gas del Estado. Betts accepted. He was a widower and had two small children to support. He began to work as a clerk and later rose to the position of representative for the company's gas distribution.

From the time he started working at LADE and Gas del Estado until the war in April 1982, the islanders close to him often asked if it was necessary for him to work for the Argentine government. "The work at LADE and at Gas del Estado allowed me to foster a very fluid relationship with the people of the continent living in Puerto Argentino," says Betts. "Through LADE I had the opportunity to leave the colony for the first time. In 1980 I travelled to Comodoro Rivadavia on commission. I realized that there was another world outside the Malvinas, with greater possibilities in the labour field, although the country was still living under the leadership of the Military Junta. Then I began to think: it seems to me that my life in the Malvinas has reached a plateau, and the only way to progress is to leave the islands and settle on the continent."

LADE and Gas del Estado had come to the islands as a result of policy agreements between Argentina and the United Kingdom, particularly through the 1971 Communications Agreement. This type of agreement contributed to the construction of a link between islanders and continental Argentines, both for those who travelled during the 1970s to provide services on the islands, and for the islanders who crossed to the mainland. "The links were harmonious," Betts says. "In the almost 11 years that the communications agreement lasted, there were no complaints, neither from islanders against continental Argentines who were living in the Malvinas, nor from continental Argentines against islanders. It was very important. Although at first there was resistance, very soon the enormous benefits that the agreements facilitated were seen: the isolation in which 'the colony' had been up to that moment was broken. There was then a great acceptance of the settlers."

The prices of goods entering the islands from the mainland were practically the same as on the mainland, while those transported from the United Kingdom were more expensive on account of greater carriage costs. Continental proximity allowed fresh fruit and vegetables to reach the islands, and not just canned goods. "At the end of the '60s, the beginning of the '70s," Betts recalls, "England was desperate to get rid of the islands: economically it was a heavy burden and they had absolutely forgotten us. Each fiscal year showed the government's growing lack of interest in the colony." So much so that, in 1970, the Falkland Islands Company decided to withdraw from service, for economic reasons, the ship that supplied the maritime supply between Montevideo and Puerto Argentino. The British government looked to Buenos Aires and began negotiations with the national government. For Argentina, an enormous opportunity opened up to set foot in the Malvinas.

Political instability and the process of decolonization
Foreign policy must be understood in relation to its contexts, both internationally and domestically. The Malvinas Question was framed, in this period, within the decolonization process undertaken by the "big five" countries which had won the Second World War and dominated the United Nations Security Council. Mainly, it was the movement of non-aligned countries[1] that gave greater impetus to this process, as they began to exert pressure on the United Nations in the context of an increasingly bipolar world.

Argentina had supported the United Nations from its creation in 1945. The foreign policy of President Arturo Illia, in 1965, was one of *rapprochement* with the region, including the United States. It also opened up new international markets, which allowed its external debt to

---

[1] The Non-Aligned Movement (NAM) is a forum for political consultation, established in 1961, that has as its foundation principles agreed at the Bandung Conference of 1955. Its main objective during the Cold War consisted in achieving the neutrality of countries in the confrontation between the antagonistic blocs of the United States and the Soviet Union.

be reduced and its economy to become more dynamic. The UK, on the other hand, faced a different situation. In the United Nations, for example, it suffered harassment from the socialists and non-aligned countries for its colonialist history and what remained of it in the present. The question of the "Falkland Islands" was part of a long list of problems facing the Labour administration of Harold Wilson, including "the British predicament in Rhodesia, and the increasing Spanish pressure on Gibraltar, which particularly concerned policy-makers in Whitehall" (González, 2009). For the United Kingdom, Argentina was:

> An important regional player that could affect the votes of other Latin American countries [...] Anglo-Argentine relations were cordial and had a rich history, despite the islands, and Buenos Aires was perceived as a more reasonable claimant than Spain, Guatemala (with respect to British Honduras) or even Venezuela (which coveted a third of the territory of British Guyana). (González, 2009)

The Islands themselves were experiencing a severe economic crisis which called into question their future self-sufficiency:

> The drop in the world price of wool threatened their only source of income [...] Solutions were difficult to find because most of the land and sheep were owned by the London-based Falkland Islands Company, whose profits went mainly to its shareholders in England. (González, 2009)

In the context of the Cold War, the United States began to develop a new policy towards the region, mainly on account of concern about the advance of communism after the Cuban Revolution of 1959. Thus, the 1966 military coup in Argentina, carried out by General Onganía, marked an important break, both in internal and foreign policy. The *de facto* government of Onganía proposed to discipline society, "adhering to the National Security Doctrine, promoted by the United States throughout Latin America [...] whose main objective was to combat the 'internal ideological enemy'" (Rapoport, 2007). This continued until the last years of the military regime, when foreign policy abandoned the idea of "ideological borders", established relations with China and Cuba, and signed a trade agreement with the Soviet Union.

Towards 1973, the external context was dominated by the oil crisis, the fall in the international trade and European protectionism. In

Argentina, democracy was returning, in a brief period overseen first by Héctor Cámpora and later by Juan Domingo Perón. An attempt was made to diversify economic and diplomatic relations "especially with the bloc of Eastern countries. Important sales were made to Cuba, granting generous credits and trying to help it against the North American blockade. Relations with the Soviet Union also deepened" (Rapoport, 2007). These policies began to be abandoned after the death of Perón in 1974, "in the government of his wife Isabel, with the rising influence of López Rega and the Peronist right and the sharpening of dissent within the ruling party" (Rapoport, 2007).

South America endured various military regimes during the period. Repressive governments had been installed in Paraguay (1954-1989), Brazil (1964-1985), Bolivia (1971-1978), Chile (1973-1980), and Uruguay (1973-1985), as well as Argentina (1976-1983). From October 1975, based on the so-called Operation Condor, a "coordination and security office" was created which functioned throughout the remainder of the 1970s and into the 1980s, and was made up of the intelligence services and security agencies of several South American countries with the shared objective of "confronting the action of guerrillas". Its method was illegal repression.

The civic-military dictatorship in Argentina, which began on 24 March 1976, created a profound transformation in society. It modified the operating rules of the financial system, generated trade openness and an accelerated de-industrialization process, along with a State terrorism policy. It was the bloodiest dictatorship in Argentine history, and it aimed to "dismantle the political, union and social resistance of the population" (Rapoport 2007). The military government proposed, on the one hand, to:

> tilt the "political pendulum" in favour of the agrarian elites and large local economic groups and external capital intermediaries, cutting off national industry and the internal market, headquarters of the strength of the labour movement and of the business sectors that support economic nationalism and the main support base of the "populist alliances" that had contributed, according to the ideological mentors of the new scheme, to the radicalization of vast sectors of the population. On the other hand, Minister Martínez de Hoz sought to readapt the economy within the framework of a type of international division of labour that was presented as a return to the sources: to Argentina "open to the world" of the agro-export era that had built the generation of 1880. (Rapoport, 2007)

Regarding foreign policy, a new type of triangular relationship emerged, with the United States on the financial and technological level, and with the Soviet Union on the commercial level.

> The latter became evident after the Soviet invasion of Afghanistan and the refusal of the Videla government to join the grain embargo against the USSR promoted by Washington, since that country was the main client of Argentina with 30% of the total exports [...] the apparent contradiction of a government that defined itself as "Western and Christian" and the deepening of economic relations with the main "enemy" power is explained by the duality of the dominant economic interests, financially and ideologically linked to the US but in which the agro-export sector had influence, needing to expand its markets to the East in the face of North American protectionism and the European Community. (Rapoport, 2009)

If the political period between 1965 and 1982 in Argentina was characterized by the political instability of democratic governments that were interrupted by military coups,[2] foreign policy on the Malvinas Question was marked at this stage by the negotiations between Argentina and the UK. This was favoured by the ongoing global decolonization process and, in particular, driven by the general recognition of the validity of United Nations Resolution 2065 (XX).

Diplomatic achievements

The United Nations was entrusted with promoting the decolonization process, which was successful in many cases in transforming colonial territories into independent states. In the 1960s, among other countries, Algeria (1962), Rwanda (1962), Jamaica (1962), Trinidad and Tobago (1962), Kenya (1963), Zambia (1964) and Barbados (1966) all became independent. The decolonization formula had two main mechanisms: the return of the territories to their original inhabitants, based on the right to self-determination of peoples; and the right to territorial integrity.

Self-determination is the "capacity that sufficiently defined populations from the ethnic or cultural point of view have to dispose of themselves and the right that a people has in a State to choose the form of govern-

---

[2] The government of Arturo Illia, which commenced in 1963, was interrupted by the military coup of 1966. The government of Héctor Cámpora and that of Juan Domingo Perón in 1973-1974, succeeded by María E. Martínez de Perón after the latter's death, was deposed by the civic-military dictatorship on 24 March 1976.

ment" (Bobbio *et al.*, 1991). However, the right to self-determination comes into tension, in some cases, with territorial integrity.

> If by virtue of the principle of self-determination a people has the power to determine its political status and the exercise of that political status necessarily supposes the existence of a territory as a framework within which public power is exercised, the effective control of the territory of a State as an attribute of that quality is necessarily linked to the exercise of the right of self-determination. In this same sense, secession as the partition of a non-autonomous territory or an independent State to become another Nation-State is the antithesis of territorial integrity. (Pastorino, 2013)

Thus, the application of the principle of self-determination was not seen as appropriate in two cases:

> This mechanism worked efficiently in all those territories in which the inhabitants – or their vast majority – were native, sometimes with the addition of a small number of citizens of the colonial power. But it got stuck in two cases: Gibraltar, where a good part of the inhabitants were British (or aspired to be) and the Malvinas, where the Hispanic and Argentine inhabitants, historically original (there were never natives in the islands), were expelled by force in 1833 and replaced by British and temporary workers. (Cisneros and Escudé, 2000)

The UK wanted the right to self-determination to apply to the Islands as well, but this was not recognized by the United Nations. "Consulting citizens from the colonial power was a contradiction in itself: self-determination corresponds to the wishes of the natives, not to those of implanted populations" (Cisneros and Escudé, 2000).

From 1833, and until 1965:

> There was a dialogue of the deaf between Argentina, which demanded the return of the islands, and the United Kingdom, which replied that it did not doubt its rights over them. In this way London managed to keep the dispute frozen and ignored by international opinion. (García del Solar, 2000)

This "dialogue of the deaf" lasted until the Argentine diplomatic achievement that marked a milestone in the debate over the Malvinas Question, namely Resolution 2065 (XX) of the United Nations General

Assembly. Following it, the UK agreed for the first time to enter into negotiations to find a peaceful solution to the dispute.

Article 1 of the resolution:

> *Invites* the Governments of Argentina and the United Kingdom of Great Britain and Northern Ireland to proceed without delay with the negotiations recommended by the Special Committee on the Situation with regard to the Implementation of the Declaration on the Granting of Independence to Colonial Countries and Peoples with a view to finding a peaceful solution to the problem, bearing in mind the provisions and objectives of the Charter of the United Nations and of General Assembly resolution 1514 (XV) and the interests of the population of the Falkland Islands (Malvinas).

Resolution 2065 (XX) granted Argentina international recognition of its historic claim and categorized the islands as a case of British colonialism. The resolution expresses the central issues of the the Malvinas Question: the existing situation is one of the forms of colonialism that must be put to an end. It is a sovereignty dispute between two states that should be addressed without delay through negotiation in order to find a peaceful resolution. To do this, the objectives and provisions of the United Nations Charter must be taken into account (including Article 33, which contains the obligation of the parties to a dispute to seek a solution first of all through negotiation; and Resolution 1514 [XV], which enshrines the principle of territorial integrity and the interests of the population of the islands, leaving aside the principle of self-determination).

Likewise, the name Islas Malvinas, in Spanish, was henceforth incorporated into all UN documents. Until then, only the Falkland Islands were listed. The solution to the dispute required considering the *interests* of the islanders, and not their *wishes*, since they were not a native people but rather an implanted population. "It is the territory that has a colonial character and not the population that occupies it, which is simply the tool of occupation" (Pastorino, 2013).

In turn, Resolution 2065 (XX) was based on Resolution 1514 (XV) of 1960, the Declaration on the granting of independence to colonial countries and peoples, which established the General Assembly's backing of the global process of decolonization. It was approved by eighty-nine votes for and none against. There were nine abstentions, one of them being the United Kingdom.

Among the grounds for this resolution, the UN belief is explained in that "the process of liberation is irresistible and irreversible and that, in order to avoid serious crises, an end must be put to colonialism and all practices of segregation and discrimination associated therewith". The ruling contains conceptual elements of great importance for Argentina and the Malvinas Question. One of them is the principle of territorial integrity that limits the principle of self-determination: "Any attempt aimed at the partial or total disruption of the national unity and the territorial integrity of a country is incompatible with the purposes and principles of the Charter of the United Nations". This principle is related to the origin of the Malvinas Question: the forceful occupation of the islands Argentina suffered in 1833 has not conferred the right to acquire the territory through the passing of time.

Another relevant pronouncement is that on the subjects of the decolonization process: "The subjection of peoples to alien subjugation, domination and exploitation constitutes a denial of fundamental human rights, is contrary to the Charter of the United Nations and is an impediment to the promotion of world peace and co-operation". Those who began to inhabit the Malvinas Islands in 1833 were not a people subject to "alien subjugation, domination and exploitation", but residents of an illegally occupying power.

In 1961 the General Assembly had created the Special Committee on Decolonization, also known as the C-24,[3] to monitor decolonization processes. This committee was where Argentine diplomacy focused its work on the search for resolutions that would promote a subsequent negotiation with the UK. It was within this body, in Subcommittee III, that the Argentine delegate, José María Ruda, had presented the fundamentals of the Argentine position. The said Subcommittee unanimously approved the following conclusions and recommendations: it confirmed that the provisions of Resolution 1514 (XV) were applicable to the territory of the Malvinas Islands; it noted the existence of a dispute between the British and Argentine governments; it recommended that the Special Committee invite both governments to enter into negotiations in order to find a peaceful solution to this problem, taking due account of the provisions and objectives of the Charter and Resolution 1514 (XV), the interests of the population and also the opinions expressed in the

[3] Its full name is The Special Committee on the Situation with regard to the implementation of the Declaration on the Granting of Independence of Colonial Countries and Peoples.

course of the general debate; and it recommended that the Special Committee invite the two aforementioned governments to inform the said Committee or the General Assembly of the results of their negotiations. In September 1964, the majority of the members of the organization favoured the Argentine position. As a consequence, the existence of a dispute over the sovereignty of the islands was accepted, Resolution 1514 (XV) was seen as applicable to the territory of the islands, and not to the population.

The year following the Ruda statement, and the recognition obtained, United Nations Resolution 2065 (XX) was agreed, during the government of President Arturo Illia, whose chancellor was Miguel Ángel Zavala Ortiz. It was approved first by the Decolonization Committee and then by the United Nations General Assembly. The then Argentine representative at the United Nations was Ambassador Lucio García del Solar.

Resolution 2065 (XX) enabled Argentina to point to the existing colonial situation in the Malvinas Islands and was a recognition of the legitimacy of its claim. Likewise, it enabled a period of negotiations, on two levels. On the one hand, there were official and informal conversations on different formulae that might resolve the underlying dispute, the sovereignty rights over the islands. On the other, understandings and cooperation in various practical aspects derived from the dispute.

> The case of Malvinas suddenly became known, like that of Gibraltar, in all the Foreign Ministries and specialized media in international relations and, second, the United Kingdom was forced to accept a process of negotiations since then. (García del Solar, 2000)

The Illia government set out to build contacts with the inhabitants of the islands, whose isolation was then considered significant.

> These contacts made it possible, on the one hand, for the islanders to see how the descendants of Anglo-Saxon immigrants had integrated and prospered in Argentina and, on the other, to guarantee respect for their cultural and political habits and the recognition of their material assets in the case that the islands were restored [...] It is the interests and not the wishes of a non-indigenous population that must be taken into account to settle a dispute originated in the violation of the territorial integrity of a country, as a consequence of a colonial situation. (García del Solar, 2000)

The first meeting to address the question of the Malvinas Islands, between the Foreign Ministers of Argentina and the United Kingdom was held in 1966. It was understood to be the beginning of negotiations. The joint communiqué of 14 January 1966, signed by Miguel Ángel Zavala Ortiz and Michael Stewart, established the commitment to find a peaceful solution to the dispute, as suggested by Resolution 2065 (XX).

The negotiations that arose from the United Nations pronouncement represented, in themselves, an important change in the European power that, since 1833, had argued that there was "nothing to discuss". They also showed the legitimacy of the Argentine position. The talks were not without difficulties. The records of the meeting between the Ministers show that "the British Secretary tried to emphasize to his counterpart that the wishes of the islanders were paramount to the United Kingdom, despite the fact that the General Assembly had not mentioned them in its Resolution, and that consequently 'It was not him who Ortiz had to persuade, but the islanders themselves'" (González, 2009).

For part of the British administration, in particular, there were vexatious problems:

> The Gibraltar and South Atlantic Department would find it complicated – domestically but also internationally – if the way in which they compromised with respect to the *wishes of the Gibraltarians* was at the same time ignored in the case of the Falkland Islands [...] This could establish a dangerous precedent, which threatened the legal position of London in the Rock (in which Great Britain did have a real strategic interest) and would have greater negative repercussions for its policies regarding Rhodesia, British Honduras and Hong Kong. (González, 2009)

The period of negotiations between 1966 and 1968 was marked by this tension between the British position, which required – because of the possible consequences in its remaining colonial territories – upholding the "wishes" of the islanders and therefore the principle of self-determination, and the Argentine position, which focused on the guarantees offered to the islanders, respecting their "interests", in the event of a restitution of sovereignty. Argentina, as stated in Resolution 2065 (XX), did not accept the islanders as a third party to the dispute, nor did it want to facilitate their veto power over the restitution of the islands (González, 2009).

Under the *de facto* government of General Onganía, both governments reached a Memorandum of Understanding of 1968. It stated:

The Government of the United Kingdom, as part of such final settlement, will recognize Argentina's sovereignty over the islands from a date to be agreed. This date will be agreed as soon as possible, after: i) the two governments have resolved the presented divergence between them as to the criteria according to which the UK government shall consider whether the interests of the islanders would be secured by the safeguards and guarantees to be offered by the Argentine Government and; ii) the Government of the United Kingdom is then satisfied that those interests are so secured. (Oliveri, 1992)

Ultimately, the Memorandum was unsuccessful.

Among the hypotheses, some authors blame Argentina for being unable to seize the moment. The inflexibility and slow pace of its diplomacy (on which see Cisneros and Escudé, 2000 and Franks, 1983), the undemocratic nature of the regime that came to power in June 1966 (Zavala Ortiz, 1977 and Calvert, 1982), and the timidity of its leadership in putting enough pressure on the British (Moreno, 1982) have been offered as explanations. But most of the work is focused on the British government. Some say that the Foreign Office was trying to sustain the reverse of the Argentine claim at the United Nations to delay negotiations (Holmberg, 1977). In his memoirs, then Foreign Minister Costa Méndez (who would be in the same post in 1982) claims that he trusted the good faith of British career diplomats but doubted the sincerity of the administration as a whole, accusing it of being responsible for the failure of the talks (Costa Méndez, 1993). Others point to persistent British interests in the islands, either in terms of access to Antarctica or as a reservoir of marine resources (Hoffmann and Hoffmann, 1984), and to individual officials and the way in which the agreement was presented to the British public (Beck, 1988). Finally, some analysts argue that the islanders themselves were largely responsible for the collapse of the negotiations, on account of the effectiveness and impact of the lobby they formed in the UK Parliament in 1968 (Ellerby, 1982). Others point to the poor negotiation margins of the British government, which had to consider the possible consequences in the rest of its colonial possessions, when it came to resolving the dispute in the Malvinas Islands (González, 2009).

Specifically, the possibility of reaching a solution became "a controversial question of British domestic politics" (Airaldi, n.d.), which led to the memorandum of agreement being abandoned. In the statement Minister Stewart made to the UK House of Commons on 11 December

1968, he said that there would be no transfer of sovereignty against the wishes of the islanders.

> Although he admitted that both governments had reached "a certain measure of understanding", he dismissed this and his words of March 1968 in the same room, saying "there is a basic divergence with respect to the insistence of the Government of HM in which there can be no transfer of sovereignty against the wishes (no longer the "interests") of the inhabitants of the Islands. (Airaldi, n.d.)

Contrary to Resolution 2065 (XX), the United Kingdom discontinued negotiations.

The following week, on 17 December 1968, the Argentine delegate to the United Nations General Assembly rejected the reasons the British government had given for not being prepared to formalize the understanding achieved. He declared that the sovereignty dispute was between Argentina and the United Kingdom and that while the interests of the population of the islands should be taken into account, their wishes should not. He recalled the principle of territorial integrity and the origin of the current population. But the negotiations had suffered a first setback.

Practical agreements

Resolution 2065 (XX), the diminishing interest the UK seemed to show in the islands and the decision of the Falkland Islands Company to withdraw from service the ship that carried supplies between Montevideo and Puerto Argentino, enabled a period of negotiations between the UK and Argentina on practical issues, which resulted in the 1971 Communications Agreement. This agreement was produced under a formula taken from the Antarctic Treaty of 1961, called the "sovereignty umbrella", which allowed that the various understandings established between the two parties, as well as the actions of third countries related to them, did not imply a modification in the respective sovereign positions.

As of the 1971 agreement, the two nations began to cooperate in the matter of regular air and maritime services, in postal, telegraphic and telephone communications, and in the fields of health, education, agriculture and technology. The agreement established a weekly air transport service for passengers, cargo and correspondence between the islands and the Argentine mainland under the responsibility of Argentina, and a regular maritime service under the responsibility of the

UK, as well as the *carte blanche*, a document without nationality identification which permitted islanders and continentals to come and go freely between the islands and the mainland without a passport stamp.

The following year, in 1972, the agreement was extended. An aerodrome was built on the islands and regular flights were commenced by the State Air Lines (LADE), which opened an office in Malvinas. Medical assistance and evacuation services were operated, a YPF fuels storage plant was installed, scholarships were awarded to islanders to study in bilingual schools on the mainland, and Spanish-language teachers came to the islands.

The Communications Agreement created an important link between the islands and the Argentine mainland. It contributed to the building of links between the islanders and the continentals on a multiplicity of subjects – education, health, work, travel and communications – and it promoted a favourable climate for a possible negotiation over sovereignty. Argentina complied with the commitments assumed, which required significant expenditure by the State. However, the UK continued to show reluctance to address the dispute.

In 1973 and 1976 the UN General Assembly approved two resolutions favourable to Argentina that complemented the principles of the 1965 pronouncement. Resolution 3160 (XXVIII) of 1973, with 116 votes in favour, none against and 14 abstentions – one of them from the UK – established that the sovereignty dispute had to be resolved in order to settle the colonial situation. Resolution 31/49 of 1976 enunciated the principle of not innovating in the matter of non-renewable natural resources while the dispute went unresolved. It was passed with 102 votes in favour, one against – the United Kingdom – and 32 abstentions.

This latter pronouncement arose in response to the first investigation into the resources of the Malvinas and their potential, carried out unilaterally by the UK on the continental shelf of the islands in 1975, within the framework of the Shackleton Mission, which was looking for hydrocarbon sediments. The 1973 oil crisis had led to the exploration for oil in spaces not controlled by the Organization of the Petroleum Exporting Countries (OPEC). One result of the Shackleton Mission was that the British began to include a new factor in bilateral negotiations: the exploration and exploitation of hydrocarbon, mining and fishing resources, which "had a direct impact on the 'wishes' and 'interests' of the islanders, at the same time that it violated what was expressed by the United Nations and what was agreed with Argentina" (Bernal, 2009).

The Shackleton Report (vol. II)

Reviews the history and geography of the archipelago and its demographic, labour and economic structure; then the different current and potential economic activities are analyzed in detail: agriculture (focused on sheep farming), fishing, mining (mainly underwater hydrocarbons), industry and crafts, transport and communications, trade and services, tourism; lastly, the social infrastructure and public services (government, housing, education, medical assistance, social security, etc.). Chapter 16 is devoted to an analysis of the Falkland Islands Company and its dominant position within the economic activity of the islands. The second volume [...] proposes what it calls "a strategy for development" and modifications, even, in the government of the islands. (Shackleton, 1976)

The results of the prospecting were positive and the areas with the highest probability of finding oil were identified. The work was carried out by two geologists from the University of Birmingham, hired by the British Crown through Parliament, and their results were published in 1976: the areas identified are exactly the areas that are currently under exploration, except for one, the most important and probably the most economically profitable, an elliptical basin that practically connects Cabo Belgrano of Gran Malvina with the city of Río Grande.

The sovereignty dispute

During Perón's government the United Kingdom was open to a dialogue on the underlying question.

The United Kingdom was perceived as a "colonialist" stronghold because of its position in Rhodesia, Namibia and South Africa and its support for the Portuguese Overseas Territories, Guinea, Angola and Mozambique. Furthermore, the West was in crisis due to rising oil prices, the United States' withdrawal from Vietnam, the appearance of the Palestine Liberation Organization, the presence of Cuba in Africa and the radicalization of the Third World. (Petrella, 2010)

In 1974, almost a decade after Resolution 2065 (XX) and three years after the practical agreements of 1971, the UK offered a solution to the sovereignty conflict. The British embassy proposed to the Argentine Foreign Minister Alberto Vignes that the official languages henceforth would be Spanish and English, the islanders would have dual citizenship, and that passports would be abolished. Governors of the islands would be appointed, alternately, by the Queen and by the Argentine President, and the two national flags would fly on the islands.

Again, the UK decided not to proceed with this alternative and, after Perón died, the British government formally withdrew the proposal. The new UK strategy, according to official British documents, was to "buy time" by delaying negotiations. To a negative external context (the oil crisis, downturns in trade, European protectionism), there was added an acute internal political conflict "marked by the existence of left-wing guerrilla movements and right-wing paramilitary forces protected by another minister, José López Rega, with a history of armed actions, kidnappings and assassinations [...] The following months saw the erosion of the government and the preparation of a 'declared' coup" (Rapoport, 2007). Along with this, the results of the Shackleton Mission of 1975, which had shown the existence of hydrocarbon resources in the disputed area, diminished the British will to work for a solution.

The next instance of negotiations for sovereignty took place during the last civic-military dictatorship, in 1980. The dominant political-diplomatic context by this time could be described as a "credible threat" situation whereby "if the negative attitude of the United Kingdom leads to a dead end, the Argentine government will be forced thoroughly to review the policy followed up to now" (Palermo, 2006). In other words, sooner or later Argentina would be "forced to say enough and do justice by its own hand" (Palermo, 2006).

According to the British historian Lawrence Freedman (2005), the British were concerned about the possibility that the dictatorship would decide to initiate military action. Among the elements that gave plausibility to this hypothesis was the direct action of the *de facto* government, in 1977 of initiating a military occupation, disguised as scientific activity, of an island in the South Thule archipelago, as well as "the recurring attitude of wanting to force the hand both in negotiations and through cooperation and integration measures between the islands and the continent" (Palermo, 2006).

On 10 and 11 September 1980, in Switzerland, a new round of negotiations between Argentina and the UK took place. This led to a trip to Buenos Aires and the Islands by the Foreign Secretary, Nicholas Ridley. The focus was a proposal from the UK similar to the one made in respect of Hong Kong: "immediate recognition of our sovereignty and a lease agreed in favour of the Crown, with growing Argentine co-administration" (Cisneros and Escudé, 2000). A session of the British Parliament on 2 December 1980 ended this alternative, after the strong opposition of Parliamentarians from both sides of the House in conjunction with the lobby of the islanders (established in 1968).

In January 1981 Argentina proposed a new round of negotiations, which was accepted the following month. Most of our knowledge of this exchange comes from the suppressed Rattenbach Report of 1983 (published by the Argentine government in 2012). In a confidential meeting on 21 February, prior to the formal negotiations, Ridley said that the islanders had a complete lack of information about the Argentine position and Argentina's urgent wish to resolve the issue. He requested the collaboration of Commodore Cavandoli in helping the islands' representatives fully to understand the Argentine position. Cavandoli's response anticipated that Argentina would reject the proposal to freeze negotiations for ten years, that Argentina had reached the limit of its patience, and that it was determined to remove all existing cooperation and withdraw from the negotiations if the issue of sovereignty was not seriously addressed.

In the round of formal negotiations that took place on 23 and 24 February 1981, Ridley sought agreement for "the freezing of the Argentine sovereignty issue for ten years". Argentina predictably rejected the proposal. A private exchange was then held between the British side and the island representatives, and then they presented the following demands to Argentina:

1) on the basis that the British have a democratic system of government and accepting that self-determination and independence of the islands was not possible, they should be offered assurances of being able to continue under a democratic regime and freedom from pressure in the future to modify such an agreement;
2) control of fishing and its exploitation in the area, and exclusion of third states, as well as the opening of the trading possibilities of the islands to investors.

Argentina responded:

a) that time was running out;
b) that the investments and the effort hitherto made by Argentina did not justify their size, largely because they had been met with distrust by the islanders;
c) that Argentina was an exemplar of compliance with its international obligations;
d) that the United Nations would be an excellent guarantor of the commitments made;
e) that any other questions were subject to agreement on the issue of restitution of sovereignty.

The round of negotiations ended with a joint statement that there had been little progress in the negotiations. The British delegation consisted of two members of the Council of the Islands, so it was assumed that the response from the Argentine side would be transmitted to the islanders. This did not happen.

Upon re-assuming the role of Foreign Minister on 22 December 1981, Nicanor Costa Méndez met with General Leopoldo Galtieri, who required him to "activate to the maximum the diplomatic actions aimed at the recognition of our sovereignty in the Malvinas, adding that he did not rule out that they had to arrive at something more than diplomacy" (Rattenbach Report, 1983). On 26 and 27 February 1982, a new round of negotiations was held in New York. For Argentina, Ambassadors Ross and Ortiz de Rozas participated; on the British side, Ministers Luce and Fearn, Ambassador Williams, and two councillors from the islands. The negotiations ended with the apparent willingness on the British side to recommend the Argentine proposal to its government. "This present-ation, called the Reactivation Proposal, favoured the establishment of a Permanent Negotiating Commission, which should meet every first week of each month, alternately in each capital, in order to maintain the continuity and momentum of the negotiation" (Rattenbach Report, 1983). On 1 March 1982, a joint communiqué was issued, which described the cordial and positive atmosphere of the meeting since the two "parties reaffirmed their decision to find a solution to the sovereignty dispute and considered in detail an Argentine proposal on procedures to achieve greater progress in this regard" (Rattenbach Report, 1983).

The following day, the military government published an expanded statement:

> Argentina has negotiated with Great Britain with patience, loyalty and good faith, for more than 15 years, within the framework indicated by the pertinent UN resolutions, the resolution of the sovereignty dispute over those islands. The new system constitutes an effective step for the prompt resolution of this dispute. Moreover, if that does not happen, Argentina maintains the right to terminate the operation of that mechanism and freely to choose the procedure that best suits its interests. (Rattenbach Report, 1983)

This statement was "effectively an ultimatum and historical explanation of what would happen less than three months later" (Cisneros and Escudé, 2000).

In the last meetings in New York prior to the war, Argentina hardened its position and urged the UK to make a decision. At that time, the island councillors, two representatives of the "hard line", were not willing to negotiate sovereignty. They accepted only practical agreements. In one of the last bilateral meetings between Argentina and the United Kingdom, prior to 2 April 1982, two commitments were agreed: the first, that the councillors would advance toward some kind of definitive agreement on the sovereignty issue if the Argentine government guaranteed certain rights. The councillors did not communicate this proposal to the islanders. The second commitment was from the Argentine government: it would not take further measures, but allow a pause and then resume negotiations the following year.

III
1982: the armed conflict

> I think that it is fine to free the Malvinas
> Islands from British domination, but it would
> be much better to free Argentina from the
> domination of its government regime.
>
> Julio F. Cortázar, 1982

Before and after

On the islands

By the beginning of April 1982, Betts had everything prepared for his departure from the Malvinas. In mid-1981, he had requested transfer from the LADE Malvinas Agency to another agency on the continent. Among the destinations the company offered him was Ushuaia, and Betts had chosen it because he wanted to familiarize himself with his province of origin, Tierra del Fuego. The trip was informally authorized, and he was waiting for the final administrative details: "On April 2, we woke up to the news that Argentine troops had landed in the vicinity of Puerto Argentino. As the islanders considered that Argentina had no legitimate right to the territory, they experienced it as an invasion. And that came in handy for the UK."

Throughout the entire armed conflict, Betts continued working for the Argentine State agencies. For LADE he took reservations and transmitted information from Puerto Argentino to Comodoro Rivadavia. At Gas del Estado, he controlled the distribution of bottled gas for private consumption. LADE flights to and from the islands, which had been regular since the agreements reached in the 1970s, were suspended as of 28 April. The measure was preventative: on 1 May the "exclusion zone" came into force.

Betts continued to go to work at the airport until 6 May. That day, the chief of the airbase, Commodore Diestre, order him to work only on administrative tasks within Puerto Argentino. The safety of the islanders should not be at risk and Puerto Argentino was the target of British naval bombardments. At Gas del Estado, he continued working until the day he left the islands.

The armed conflict distanced him from his brothers, who participated in it on the British side. His elder brother joined the Falkland Islands militia. The younger brother, who had travelled to the United Kingdom

46

several years before, served in the Merchant Navy, and during the months of the conflict remained on a tanker that supplied British units.

On 10 May 1982, the United Kingdom sank the cargo ship *Isla de los Estados*. Twelve of Betts's friends, whom he had met on other Argentine ships that had provided supplies to the islands since 1974, were killed. Betts left the islands on 26 June 1982, on the last voyage of the *Bahía Paraíso* ship, which left Puerto Argentino carrying three hundred wounded Argentine men who had been in the Malvinas hospitals. In the city of Santa Fe, waiting for him, was his son Pablo, who had travelled to the continent after the educational agreements of the 1970s. He was in his second year of high school.

On the mainland
Everyone calls Michael O'Byrne Mike. He is a descendant of Islanders and an inhabitant of Río Gallegos, province of Santa Cruz. Mike's maternal great-great-grandfather, Rudd, was a Scotsman who had come to the Islands in 1845 in search of a better life. Years later, his children first crossed to Punta Arenas and then settled in Río Gallegos in 1885, enthused by Governor Moyano's proposals. Almost a century later, when Mike asked his girlfriend to marry him, he did not imagine that the ceremony would take place in the middle of the Malvinas war, much less that the party planned and organized in detail at the British Club of Río Gallegos, of which his father-in-law was the President, was going to have to be suspended.

Since its foundation in 1911, a portrait of the British monarch had dominated one of the walls of the club. During the war, the Directors' Committee decided to call the press and the authorities. They took the portrait down, put it away, and put a picture of General San Martín in its place. During the war there were some tensions in the city among the British descendants, who were already fourth- and fifth-generation Argentines, although there were no major conflicts. Until the armed conflict, Mike's wife worked along with about twenty others at Shell Hydrocarbons, an Anglo-Dutch company established in 1978 in Río Gallegos for offshore oil development. "Imagine how one of these companies works," says Mike, "all over the world, in all kinds of political contexts, and what their contingency plans are like. On April 1, they predicted what would happen. On April 3 they began to mobilize. And on April 4, no one was left. They left the Argentines to wind things up. In the entire country, by the way, there were no foreigners who worked for the company."

The Foreign Policy

Between 1965 and 1982, the Argentine and British governments held intermittent negotiations on the question of sovereignty:

> But the abandonment by Argentina of the mandate received from the United Nations to negotiate the settlement of the dispute peacefully, as a result of the military occupation of the Malvinas, was used by British diplomacy unilaterally to terminate the negotiations, in fact reverting to the situation prior to 1965. (García del Solar, 2000)

The 74-day conflict, triggered by the *de facto* presidency of Lieutenant General Leopoldo Fortunato Galtieri and by the government of Prime Minister Margaret Thatcher, resulted in the deaths of 649 Argentines and the deaths of 255 British, with more than a thousand wounded.

Contrary to what was expected by the *de facto* government, the United States aided the UK in the logistical aspects of the war. Among other actions, on 3 April the US authorized the UK to use Ascension Island as a logistics base. On 30 April, for example, after an attempt to mediate between the parties, the American Foreign Secretary, Alexander Haig, announced the suspension of all military exports to Argentina, the suspension of credits from the Export-Import Bank and the suspension of guarantees for the purchase of Argentine products. The Argentine military government consequently had to extend its participation in forums that were not, until then, considered related, such as the Movement of Non-Aligned Countries, led by Cuba since 1979. Latin America had not hitherto been a central axis of its foreign policy. The *de facto* government "militarily underestimated the British, the American position was not understood and the expected support of the Soviets was not obtained. Only the Latin American countries were in solidarity with the Argentine cause" (Rapoport, 2007).

The armed conflict also ended the internal debate within the UK. "From then on, no one, either in the Foreign Office or anywhere else, has proposed to discuss sovereignty with Argentina. The British argue that there was a war, started by us, and that they won it, end of story. For the British, victory confers rights" (Cisneros and Escudé, 2000). For Argentina this was not so, and it has continued with its claim. Nor was it so for the United Nations, which has continued to promote resolutions from the international community, year after year, urging dialogue between the two countries. In November of that same year of 1982, the General Assembly adopted Resolution 37/9, which once again asked the Argentine and British governments to resume negotiations in order to find a peaceful solution to the sovereignty dispute as soon as possible. In addition, it requested the Secretary General to undertake a renewed mission to assist the parties in the requested compliance.

The military conflict had obviously hindered progress on the dispute, and damaged the relationship with the United Kingdom and with the islanders. Freedman (2005) argues:

> Had the war not existed, the islands would have become progressively unviable for the United Kingdom. They were losing population annually, starting from a very small base, and eventually something was going to have to be done. But by forcing the issue in this way, the Argentines made the UK decide to invest in the islands, to take an interest in them and to take care of them as it had not done before.

The implications of the conflict have been widely studied by, among others, León Rozitchner, Rosana Guber, Federico Lorenz, Vicente Palermo, and Vicente Berasategui. Understanding the armed conflict requires framing it in the state terrorism of the last military dictatorship. The *de facto* government saw its chances of continuity in a victory. Defeat in the war consequently accelerated the end of the civic-military dictatorship. The war was the only one to which Argentina was party in the twentieth century. As for foreign policy, the achievement of Argentine diplomacy in 1965 which had given impetus to negotiations on the sovereignty dispute and on practical matters, the war launched by the last military dictatorship provided a justification for the British to put an end to negotiations. Likewise it was the only moment, since 1833 and for more than 180 years, in which the search for the resolution of the dispute did not proceed peacefully. It also redefined the links between the continental population and the islanders.

IV
1983-1989: the distance

The return to democracy

The year 1983 marked a return to democracy in Argentina. The government of President Raúl Alfonsín abandoned the very notion of conflict with the countries of the region in its early years. The new government "made foreign policy a double instrument to reposition the country in front of international society and strengthen the government system" (Merke, 2010). If Argentina was henceforth conceived of as a western, non-aligned and developing country, the organizing principle of Alfonsín's foreign policy was "the protection and consolidation of democracy" (Russell, 2003). Actions were taken both to protect the institutional order and to promote the country's presence in the international arena.

> The search for support for the new democratic regime among European governments, particularly those with a social-democratic orientation, the continuation of Argentine-Soviet relations at the economic and diplomatic levels, and a *rapprochement* with Latin American countries, were some of its main axes. An attempt was also made to establish what was defined as "a mature relationship" with the United States. (Paradiso, 1993)

The strengthening of Latin American integration took place through the Latin American Integration Association (ALADI) and the Latin American and Caribbean Economic System (SELA). Faced with the Central American crisis, Argentina sought to establish itself as a protagonist on the regional scene, defending the principle of non-intervention and the legal equality of States (Paradiso, 1993).

For Argentina, *rapprochement* with Brazil was an instrument to break its political and economic marginalization in the international sphere. From the outset, efforts were made to agree positions on issues considered priorities such as external debt, the Malvinas Question and the Central American crisis. For Brazil, this made it possible to put aside any threat of conflict inherited from the past, a necessary step to consolidate a space of freedom and prestige in the international system (Hirst, 1991). There began with Brazil "a process of cooperation in the economic and nuclear fields that laid the foundations of MERCOSUR" (Merke, 2010). After a meeting in Foz de Iguazú on 30 November 1985, Presidents Raúl Alfonsín and José Sarney signed the Joint Declaration on Nuclear Policy, by which they reaffirmed the peaceful purposes of their respective nuclear programmes and resolved to step up cooperation in that field.

As well as seeking peace with neighbours and democracy in the region, a human rights policy was promoted. The Alfonsín government and social and human rights organizations, such as Grandmothers of Plaza de Mayo and Mothers of Plaza de Mayo, promoted the prosecution of members of the Military Junta.[1] Likewise, Argentina supported the International Criminal Court from the beginning (Merke, 2010).

On the economic level, Argentina had suffered the consequences of the economic policies imposed by the civic-military dictatorship, including de-industrialization, unemployment and social fragmentation. These economic difficulties recurred throughout the period of the Alfonsín government, which culminated in the hyperinflationary crisis of 1989. Despite the initial efforts of the government, "the problems generated by external indebtedness, economic stagnation and inflation could not be resolved. A new monetary unit, the Austral, was created, which failed in the attempt to give economic agents greater confidence and instead unleashed an acute hyperinflationary process that brought down the government" (Rapoport, 2007).

Arrival

Upon arriving on the mainland, Alejandro Betts requested from the Córdoba Civil Registry his identity document and that of his son Pablo, who had been studying in the Province of Santa Fe since the beginning of 1981, which he received in October 1982. "Now I have *Patria*. Which is my country? The one of my children, that of my grandchildren, the one that was of my parents and my grandparents, is Argentina. Britain never recognized me as a citizen; I was an instrument that they needed for their illegitimate stay in the territory." The law in 1927 stated that any person native to the Malvinas Islands should be considered Argentine, consistent with the assumed legitimacy of Argentine sovereignty over the archipelago. "I got off at Punta Alta, in Puerto Belgrano, and I went from there to Rosario, in Santa Fe province, because Pablo was studying in his second year at the Liceo Aeronáutico Militar in the town of Funes, 30

---

[1] The Alfonsín government, after trials of the military leaders that led to guilty verdicts, faced armed uprisings and finally yielded to military pressure, decreeing the Leyes de Punto Final (1986) and Obediencia Debida (1987) laws, now derogated. Those laws prevented those responsible for crimes against humanity from being tried; this situation changed in 2003 with the National Law 25.799 (2003), promoted by the government of Néstor Kirchner.

kilometres away." Starting with the agreements of the 1970s, the Argentine government had offered scholarships to islander students. As an employee of LADE, Betts had given Pablo the opportunity to complete his studies at the Liceo.

For the first two years after the war, Betts had almost no ties to his family on the islands. He exchanged only a few letters with his mother. His brothers made no attempt to contact him. Pablo continued studying in Santa Fe and Alejandro decided to go to live in Córdoba, where LADE also operated and where could be close to his son. In those years he learned Spanish.

Legal validity of the dispute

Victory does not give rights unless the defeated party abandons its claim. There were in this period successive Argentine attempts to re-establish relations with the UK. After the war, the British wanted to ignore the dispute, but Argentina persisted at the General Assembly of the United Nations and achieved, year after year, pronouncements that reiterated support for Resolution 2065 (XX). Between 1982 and 1988, the General Assembly annually adopted similar resolutions, urging negotiation between the parties (Resolution 37/9; Resolution 38/12; Resolution 39/6; Resolution 40/21; Resolution 41/40; Resolution 42/19; and Resolution 43/25). Likewise, the Special Committee on Decolon-ization has since 1983 continually endorsed similar pronouncements. The outcome of the war did not change the legal status of the dispute.

However, the conflict of 1982 led to a significant change in the relationship between the UK government and the islanders. The natives of the islands had never been recognized as a full UK citizens. To travel to the UK, for example, they had had obtain a 90-day tourist visa. As a result of the war, the United Kingdom granted citizenship to native islanders in 1983, for the first time in 150 years of occupation, through the British Nationality (Falkland Islands) Act. It was only in 2002 that British nationality law was modified for all its overseas territories.

In his inaugural speech to Congress on 10 December 1983, Alfonsín referred to the Malvinas issue:

In the case of the Malvinas, South Georgia and South Sandwich Islands, our unwavering object is and will always be their recovery and the definitive affirmation of our nation's right to its sovereign territorial integrity. At this point we are inflexible and sovereignty is a precondition of negotiation. We will promote the recovery of these island territories and their definitive integration into the sovereignty of the Nation, demanding with energy and determination compliance with the current resolutions of the United Nations General Assembly that call for direct negotiation on all aspects. Meanwhile we denounce once again, as a serious threat to the security of the Argentine Republic and the entire region, the installation of the military and nuclear fortress established by the United Kingdom in the Malvinas Islands, as well as the "exclusion zone" declared by that country.

He thus maintained as a priority negotiations for sovereignty rights over the islands as a prior step to agreeing on other matters.

The first of the attempts to improve relations with the UK government after the war ended at the frustrated talks in Berne, Switzerland in 1984. There were no diplomatic relations at the time. The perspective of the Argentine government was that it was willing to enter dialogue but only if all the issues were included, that is, as long as the question of sovereignty was retained. Margaret Thatcher's administration was uncompromising on that matter. The British were prepared to discuss only practical matters. Consequently negotiations, including those related to the re-establishment of diplomatic relations, came to a standstill.

The Argentine government adopted multilateral negotiation as a new strategy, mainly in three international forums: the Organization of American States, the Non-Aligned Group and the United Nations. The support obtained did not change the British position and Argentina continued to seek bilateral negotiates with the UK. At the same time, the UK continued to take new actions that deepened tensions between the two countries. In 1984, the Falkland Islands Development Corporation (FIDC) was created on the islands in order to diversify the economy, improve infrastructure and encourage selective immigration. Land redistribution was also increased. In 1985 the United Kingdom drew up a new "Constitution" for the islands, which was intended to give islanders greater control over their internal affairs. That same year, for the first time, the UK tried to introduce two amendments in the United Nations aimed at giving prominence to the principle of self-determination, which were rejected by a large majority.

The next attempt at *rapprochement* took place in 1986, "promoted by the United States, given the increase in tensions due to the unilateral decision of the British government to create the Falklands Interim Conservation Zone (FICZ), to exercise absolute control of fishing activities within a 150-mile radius around the islands" (García del Solar, 2000). By 1989 the world context had changed. This year marked the end of the Cold War, of East-West confrontation and the politics of blocs. The scene was different. The active Argentine work in the Decolonization Committee offered new possibilities for discussions with the British. It pursued a different approach. "This did not seem illusory in light of the prevailing international climate, the good relationship with the United Kingdom, the specific bilateral support received by Argentina, and because it was also consistent with practice in matters of transferring territories" (Petrella, 2010).

Between 1986 and 1988 there was a frequent exchange of papers between Buenos Aires and London through the US State Department, which laid the foundations for subsequent conversations. The normalization of diplomatic relations was effected by the Madrid Agreements of 1989-90. A new period in seeking a resolution to the Malvinas Question began. The new strategy consisted of approaching the UK government and the islanders, while maintaining the legal claim in the United Nations. The 1982 war had significantly changed the situation:

> The diplomatic strategy was to try to resume practical arrangements in the style of the 1971 accords, although in the framework of a very unfavourable scenario. The memory of the war and the threats of the use of force were far from having healed [...] It was essential to have a relationship with the economic activity of the islands to generate new bonds of mutual knowledge and recreate a spirit of trust. (Petrella, 2010)

V
The policy of *rapprochement*

> About the British: think this. They defeated Napoleon,
> the Bourbons, Bismarck, they liquidated the Austro-
> Hungarian Empire, the Turkish Empire and Hitler,
> and saw Stalin through. It is not just any country. Then
> you have to put yourself in the head of the other.
>
> Interview with Fernando Petrella (2013)

The end of the twentieth century

The fall of the Berlin Wall on 9 November 1989 symbolized a profound
epochal change: the end of the Cold War or, as the British historian, Eric
Hobsbawm (2001) characterized the year 1989, the "end of the short
twentieth century".

The international scene changed. The UK was a prestigious actor in
the system and its close relationship with the United States strengthened
it. "The NAM was completely appeased and its members worried about
attracting investment from Western countries. The countries of the
former socialist orbit, with Russia at the head, sought a *rapprochement*
with the West without conditions" (interview with Fernando Petrella,
2013). As for Argentina, its participation in the first Gulf War and in
peacekeeping operations enabled informal dialogue with the UK.
Likewise, "the climate for foreign investments visibly improved, a
circumstance taken advantage of by the UK and other Europeans [...] The
economic opportunities and the 'business climate' Argentina offered in
the years 1990-1995, also made its contribution to the *rapprochement*
between the two countries" (interview with Fernando Petrella, 2013).

The Malvinas Question was newly understood in the changed
scenario.

> Menem's priority was to re-establish diplomatic relations with the
> United Kingdom because of the role the United Kingdom played in the
> western alliance. Politics must be seen globally [...] when the Berlin
> Wall fell, all that remained was the western constellation. There was
> nothing to discuss, there was no non-alignment: either you are friends
> with these guys or you are going to a cesspool. (Interview with
> Fernando Petrella, 2013)

During this period, the development of MERCOSUR was also promoted,
mainly in commercial aspects. It also adhered to the Tlatelolco Treaty of

1969 (which prohibited Latin American states from acquiring nuclear weapons) and Non-Proliferation Treaties. As for Chile, Argentina "offered its support to the opponents of the dictatorial regime of Augusto Pinochet and resolved the Beagle issue" (Merke, 2010).[1]

The new government of Argentina, under the presidency of Carlos Menem, had taken office in a context of hyperinflationary crisis at the same time that the international scene was transformed.

> With the euphoria caused by the fall of the Berlin Wall and the Soviet bloc and the process of financial globalization driven by new technologies and the expansion of speculative markets, there was also an overabundance of capital in the north. This coincided, in turn, with the liberalizing policies advocated by the so-called Washington Consensus and with the coming to power in Argentina of Carlos Menem. (Rapoport, 2007)

The Washington Consensus was promoted in the region and was based on the "recipes" of international organizations such as the World Bank and the International Monetary Fund.

The economic model promoted in Argentina during the 1990s focused on the downsizing of the State, the privatization of public companies, financial services, trade openness and an increase in foreign debt. All of this took place, under the Convertibility Law, which established the exchange parity of the national currency with the US dollar. The consequences were the destruction of industry and of a significant proportion of jobs (Basualso, 2006). The neoliberal model caused a prolonged crisis from 1998-2002 and serious social, political and economic conflicts.

Trade with the islands

Mike O'Byrne travelled to the Malvinas Islands in 2001 to buy wool, to then process and export from Argentina. But he also took the opportunity to rediscover his family history: Rudd, his maternal great-great-grandfather, is buried in the Darwin cemetery. To this day, his family's presence persists on the islands. The crossing on the San Carlos River, on Soledad Island, bears the name "Vado de Rudd", in homage to its ancestor. Mike's trip to the islands lasted a week. In that time, he toured the two main islands, and visited approximately forty-five commercial

---

[1] The Beagle issue was a long-running border dispute between Chile and Argentina.

establishments. He stayed at the Port Howard ranch where, during the war, a battalion of around 800 Argentine soldiers had been billeted. At present, a shed on that farm houses a war museum full of Argentine paraphernalia: *Jockey* cigarette packs, espadrilles, *Flecha* sneakers – which the conscripts wore in the middle of winter – an ejected seat from an aeroplane and a pilot's helmet. To the south, there is a crashed Mirage plane, lying in the middle of the field, seen as one passes on the nearby road.

On the islands, Mike was generally treated well, there was interest in his family history and business propositions. The islanders loaded the wool to be sent to London through an intermediary who as broker benefited most from the transactions. They sold it and got paid, and although they didn't own the business, this new alternative was a good opportunity. Of the few tense situations that Mike experienced on the islands there was one with a retired British serviceman.

The old establishments of the islands, which over the decades were distributed among different families after the Falkland Islands Company was subdivided, had the same structure as those of the continent. The sheds, the ceilings, the sheets, the wood, the light fixtures, the machinery, the motors, the presses, were all identical. "It is as if they had loaded one ship after another," says Mike. "One for Chile, one for the islands, one for Río Gallegos. For example, one of the machines at Cabo Buen Tiempo, a Shaw from 1911 that still works, is the same one that is in the Viamonte ranch in Tierra del Fuego, the same one that is by Río Gallegos in Port Howard, and in Darwin."

Policy Development

In 1989, relations between Argentina and the UK were re-established by the Madrid Agreements. The cessation of hostilities was agreed, consular relations were re-affirmed, a working group was created with the objective of avoiding incidents in the military field by promoting cooperation and trust, commercial and financial relations were stimulated by eliminating all restrictions imposed as of 1982 , and air and maritime communications were resumed. From 1989 until 2003, policy focused on the *rapprochement* and deepening of relations with the UK and with the islanders.

One of the thrusts of the government's policy focused on the promotion of various provisional understandings, signed under the formula of the so-called "sovereignty umbrella", which were expected to be beneficial for both countries. In the Joint Declaration of the Argentine and British governments of Madrid of 19 October 1989, it was agreed, among other issues, that the meetings would not be interpreted as indicating a change in either, or any other, country's position about the sovereignty or territorial and maritime jurisdiction of the islands. The importance of establishing this mechanism was manifested not only in the possibility of promoting agreements that could be of interest to Argentina and the United Kingdom, but also implied that the UK once again recognized, after the conflict of 1982, that there was still a sovereignty dispute. The mechanism was copied from the formula that Argentina had brought to the Antarctic Treaty and also proposed in the 1970s agreements, although the context was different. The 1971 agreements had been promoted after the diplomatic achievement of Resolution 2065 (XX) in the context of the decolonization process; the understandings reached at this stage were framed in the attempt to re-establish relations with the UK. Thus, between 1989 and 2003, 47 provisional understandings were signed by the two countries, of which more than a third (17) were to do with practical matters on the islands. The policy of the 1990s assumed that a discussion on sovereignty would take place at the end of a path of practical understandings.

> There was no other way to conduct a new Malvinas policy than to prepare the ground. First, we cooperate for fifty years and in the end sovereignty will fall like a ripe fruit, that is the idea [...] There will be some solution that is sufficiently unsatisfactory for both parties. Di Tella said that good agreements are those in which both parties are equally unsatisfied. The formula is: sovereignty at the end and not at the beginning; cooperation at the beginning and not at the end, not contingent on sovereignty. And umbrellas in the meantime. (Interview with Andrés Cisneros, 2013)

This was a reversal of the previous approach, in which sovereignty had been prioritised by Argentina and discussion of other matters seen as conditional upon it. According to Domingo Cavallo, Minister of Foreign Affairs from 1989 to 1991, "our remote geographical position had been aggravated by our progressive economic and political deterioration [...] we needed dialogue and negotiation in order to create the conditions that would one day allow us fully to regain sovereignty over the Malvinas within current international legislation" (Cavallo, 1996).

The Report of the Argentine-British Working Group on Fisheries was approved; the South Atlantic Working Group was created; the visit of the relatives of those killed in combat to the Puerto Darwin cemetery, sponsored by the International Red Cross, was agreed upon; the embassies in Buenos Aires and London were re-opened on 26 February 1990. On the last day of March 1990, the British government proceeded to lift the military protection zone around the islands.

On 1 February 1991, Guido Di Tella became Chancellor. At the Decolonization Committee meeting of 14 July 1993, Di Tella stated that "the establishment of direct links with the islanders (that is to say, formal and informal without British intermediaries) has become a central point of our policy on the subject [as] their opinions have a fundamental influence on the British position". In 1994, the reform of the National Constitution incorporated a clause on the Malvinas Question which ratified the importance that the peaceful recovery of the islands has for Argentina. According to the First Transitory Clause:

> The Argentine Nation ratifies its legitimate and inalienable sovereignty over the Malvinas, South Georgia and South Sandwich Islands and the corresponding maritime and island spaces, as they are an integral part of the national territory.
>
> The recovery of the said territories and the full exercise of sovereignty, respecting the way of life of its inhabitants and in accordance with the principles of International Law, constitute a permanent and inalienable objective of the Argentine people. (Constitución Nacional, 1994)

In other words, it was State policy that the claim for sovereignty remained firm, that the search for the resolution of the controversy would be carried out only in a peaceful way, and that the way of life of the islanders would be respected in any recovery of the territories.

In 1998 Di Tella wrote to the British Foreign Secretary Robin Cook. The letter affirmed that it was "the Argentine intention to once again maintain with the islanders a normal and habitual relationship that, over time, facilitates the administration of our differences and the progressive understanding between us". It makes explicit that the sovereignty discussion would come after a series of practical steps and agreements.

The well-known shipment in 1998 of 600 *Winnie-the-Pooh* books to the islanders – one for each family – was framed within this agenda, and each came with a greeting card from Di Tella, which read: "My dear neighbour, these stories, full of warmth, simplicity and wit, can help build a sense of family between us [...] this year has been full of promising events for our common future and I am confident that we shall be able to move forward together a fruitful relationship".

In this end-of-the century period, issues relating to flights, de-mining in the Malvinas Islands, the analysis of the toponymy and the construction of a Monument to the Argentine Fallen were agreed. There were problematic agreements, largely because of unilateral British actions, on fishing and hydrocarbons and the delimitation of the continental shelf.

The Argentine-British Working Group on South Atlantic Issues met in November 1990 and adopted a Joint Declaration by which it was agreed to initiate cooperation in order to contribute to the conservation of fishery resources. As a result, the South Atlantic Fisheries Commission was established, as well as the temporary total prohibition of commercial fishing by vessels of any flag in the area described in its annexe, located between latitude 45° and 60° south-east of Malvinas and covering an expanse of 205,000 square kilometres.

The Commission was to monitor the fishing ban and report developments to governments. It also had among its functions to receive from both States the information available on the operations of the fleets, the statistics on catches and on the analysis of the stocks of the most significant species, to evaluate the information received and transmit recommendations to both governments, and to propose joint scientific research.

Despite the understanding, and even before it, there had been unilateral British acts, which included the establishment of purported maritime jurisdictions around the Islands in 1986 and 1990, and around the South Georgia and the South Sandwich Islands in 1993, the sale of fishing licences since 1987, the unilateral lifting in 1994 of the total temporary prohibition of fishing stipulated in the proscribed area and in the area to the West of that.

Hydrocarbons were controversial from the beginning. The understanding would offer commercial opportunities to Argentine companies of the Patagonian region in particular. Argentina would benefit from activities carried out in areas subject to the sovereignty dispute until both parties resolved it. The understanding and its implementation did not imply, nor could they be interpreted, as an acceptance of the alleged British right to call for a bids for the exploration and exploitation of hydrocarbons in the maritime areas surrounding the islands. The United Kingdom encouraged a unilateral and immediate opening of tenders for large companies to explore the islands' coast in search of oil and gas. Shell, Agip and other multinational companies spent more than 150 million US dollars in exploration. In theory, the agreement would allow for the joint exploration by both countries of a defined area around the islands, but as soon as the understanding was signed, the British activity began without Argentine participation.

The first meeting of the Commission on Hydrocarbons in the Southwest Atlantic took place in March 1996. The climate was tense. "By 1998 it was clear that the block awards made by the British had not borne fruit, so London announced an open-door policy in the disputed area. On the direct instructions of Foreign Minister Di Tella, at the July 1999 Commission session, this was categorically rejected. The fate of the Hydrocarbons Commission seemed negatively sealed" (Petrella, 2010). The last meeting of the Commission, which was to discuss the scope of the agreement, was on 24 July 2000, when a "period of reflection" was begun, from which it never resumed.

In the five years between the signing of the understanding and the last meeting of the commission, the British authorities called for tenders for the exploration and exploitation of areas of the maritime subsoil under dispute. Companies from important developed countries came forward, arguing that the legal security clause contained in the Declaration in its Article 6 protected them. Interest had grown with rising oil prices and continued until their crash in 1998, when it fell to 10 US dollars a barrel, reducing the profitability and attractiveness of exploration (Cámpora, 2000). The price of a barrel rose again in 1999 and a change of intention from the UK was no longer expected.

The unilateral actions developed by the United Kingdom since 1991 in the field of hydrocarbons are a regrettable reflection of this mistrust. It is enough to cite an example to verify the absence of good faith. In October 1995, a month after the Joint Declaration of Cooperation on offshore activities in the Southwest Atlantic was agreed, it unilaterally announced the opening of a round of licenses for the exploration and exploitation of hydrocarbons to the north and southwest of the Islands. In 1996, it granted seven licences for offshore hydrocarbon production to the north of the island. The existence of a bilateral cooperation framework did not stop the United Kingdom in 2000 from enacting the "Offshore Petroleum (Licensing) Regulations 2000" or granting licenses for the exploration and production of hydrocarbons in ten blocks located to the south and east of the Islands. Despite Argentine efforts, the cooperation agreement was systematically distorted by these unilateral actions. Even the central provisions were a matter of divergent interpretation. (García Moritán, 2010)

The 1982 Convention on the Law of the Sea provided for the creation of the Commission on the Limits of the Continental Shelf. At the time of ratifying the convention, on 1 December 1995, the Argentine Republic made "a declaration by which it expressed its reservation on the Question of the Malvinas Islands" (García Moritán, 2010). The National Law of Argentina No. 24.815 (1997), created the National Commission for the Outer Limit of the Continental Shelf (COPLA), which drew up the final proposal, seeking to consolidate the exercise of sovereignty rights on natural resources to be found in "1,000,000 square kilometres [...] a reservoir of energy and mineral resources of great strategic and economic importance" (García Moritán, 2010). On 8 and 20 June 2001, the Argentine Republic and the United Kingdom concluded an agreement for on the exchange of information about the preparatory activities for the respective presentations before the Commission on the Limits of the Continental Shelf.

Another important understanding of the period was that on Communications, based on the Joint Declaration of 14 July 1999, which addressed various practical matters. It re-established access for continental Argentines to the islands, on the presentation of valid passports. The passport was stamped by the British authorities upon arrival on the islands. Under the sovereignty formula, this had no legal effects regarding the substantive dispute, although symbolically it was not equivalent to the *carte blanche* arrangement of the 1970s, which had not required the stamping of passports. A regular weekly flight between the islands and the continent started to be operated by the Chilean company LAN Airlines, between Punta Arenas and the islands with two stopovers – one in each direction – in Río Gallegos.

In turn, through a new understanding of February 2001, the flights of private civil aircraft and the navigation of private vessels from the continental territory to the islands and from the Islands to the continent were placed under the "sovereignty umbrella". The British, outside the understanding of communications, began to request additional flight permits from Argentina. Argentina gave permission and charter flights flew over the Argentine mainland.

The reluctance of the British to resolve the de-mining issue "derived from the fact that the UK did not wish to favour a new Argentine presence in the territory, whatever the reason and however reasonable it may seem" (Petrella, 2010). Negotiations culminated at the end of 2001 with an agreement to carry out a feasibility study on de-mining in the Malvinas, aimed at compliance with the obligations assumed by Argentina in the 1997 [Ottawa] Convention on de-mining, use, storage, production and transfer of antipersonnel mines and their destruction. The study was carried out by both governments through a joint working group.

The Declaration of 14 July 1999 expressed the will of the Argentine government to analyze the toponymy of the Malvinas Islands. On 10 November 2000, the Inter-ministerial Commission for the Analysis of Toponymy in the Malvinas Islands was created. The Directorate of Geography of the National Geographic Institute, in conjunction with the Toponymy section of the Naval Hydrography Service, drew up a standardized nomenclature of place names of the Malvinas Islands from scale cartography, which contains, among other data, specific terms, generic terms, geographic coordinates and locations.

Third party international support for the Argebtine position was also sought. In 1992, for the first time, Chile made reference at presidential level to the Argentine claim for the islands, as did Mexico and Colombia, at the same level. On 25 June 1996, the member countries of MERCOSUR, Bolivia and Chile, expressed in the Declaration of Potrero de los Funes their support for the legitimate rights of Argentina in the sovereignty dispute. It was reiterated in the Declaration of Asunción in June 1999.

1999-2003

The policy on the Malvinas Question did not change significantly during the governments of the Alliance under the presidencies of Fernando de la Rúa (1999-2001) and Eduardo Duhalde (2002-2003). With some alteration in the tone of the dispute – especially in relation to the islanders and the intervention in one of the understandings – the position of both governments was, mainly, a continuation of the policy initiated during the 1990s. The main differences were presented in relation to the islanders and in the hydrocarbon commission.

The Argentine crisis in 2001 led to the early departure of the government chaired by Fernando de la Rúa. In the transition between the end of his government and the beginning of Duhalde's, which lasted two weeks between 20 December 2001 and 2 January 2002, five presidents succeeded each other.[2] Among them, Adolfo Rodríguez Saá declared the suspension of the payment of the foreign debt. The British perceived Argentina's weakness and hardened their position, extending

---

[2] Fernando de la Rúa ruled from December 1999 to December 2001; Ramón Puerta from 20-23 December 2001; Adolfo Rodríguez Saá from 23-30 December 2001; Eduardo Camano formed the assembly that appointed the next president; and Eduardo Duhalde was interim president, from 2 January 2002 to 25 May 2003.

unilateral actions. In Duhalde's new government, Malvinas was not among the foreign policy priorities.

In 2000, a joint declaration was signed with Paraguay, in support of the legitimate rights of Argentine sovereignty over the Malvinas. Joint declarations were also promoted in that year – at the bilateral level – with the presidents of Chile, Venezuela, Bolivia, Mexico and Colombia, in support of Argentine rights. In the same year, a joint communiqué was issued by the Foreign Ministers of Argentina and Russia, Adalberto Rodríguez Giavarini and Igor Ivanov, in which they reiterated that the question of the Malvinas Islands should be resolved through negotiations between the Argentine Republic and the UK. In 2001, a communiqué was promoted by the Foreign Ministers of Argentina and Peru in support of Argentine rights, as well as a joint communiqué from Argentina and Saint Lucia, issued by President De la Rúa and Prime Minister Kenny Davis Anthony, with the support of the English-speaking Caribbean, and a statement signed by De la Rúa and the Prime Minister of Grenada.

The Ibero-American Summits that bring together the Heads of State of the nineteen Ibero-American countries, together with Spain and Portugal, have reiterated annually since 2000 the need for Argentina and the United Kingdom to resume negotiations as soon as possible. The first South American Summit of 2000, adopted a declaration noting the colonial situation of the Malvinas Islands and a agreed on the need for both parties to resume negotiations. At a meeting of the Central American Integration System (SICA), on 4 December 2000, a declaration was issued whose paragraph 27 reaffirmed the same need.

Cousins

Georgina Gleadell is a daughter of islanders and resident of San Julián, province of Santa Cruz. Her English great-grandparents had settled in the Malvinas in 1853. Years later, they crossed to the continent with their children, when her father, born in Port Darwin, was a 9-year-old boy. Over the years, some of her uncles returned to live on the islands; her parents stayed on the continent. Towards the end of the 1990s, Georgina was interested in communicating with her relations who lived in the Malvinas. Through the internet, she contacted John Fowler, an islander who had been a superintendent of education, who helped her in the search.

Her cousin, Lisa Watson, was then the editor of the *Penguin News*, the local newspaper, so reaching her was easy. Georgina wrote to her and they had a dialogue by mail for a time in which they discussed the possibility of a meeting. A short time later, Georgina travelled to the islands. John received her and took her to meet her cousin. But the first attempt was thwarted without much explanation. A few days later, the same thing happened. "On the third attempt," recalls Georgina, "in a mixture of Spanish and English, John said to me, 'I have to be honest with you, the men of the Watson family do not want Lisa to meet you. They are very anti-Argentine.'" She then decided not to cross to the other island, where Ian Gleadell, her paternal cousin, lived. Some time later, she received an email from John. Ian had told him, "What a pity she didn't come, I did want to meet her."

VI
2003-2015: the *firmness* policy

Emerging countries and regional integration

The national government that took office in 2003, under the presidency of Néstor Kirchner, marked a change of course. The government's decisions were oriented towards the recovery of State capacities and the redirection of foreign policy towards Latin America. The new government:

> redefined and recovered the active role of the State in the design and implementation of the development model. The proposed model was supported mainly by a process of reindustrialization and import substitution that designated the domestic market the main axis of growth. It was also based on a State willing to carry out the infrastructure works, investment promotion and federal and regional integration necessary for the process to be consolidated over time [...] Outwardly, the country advanced in the processes of regional integration, reserving high degrees of autonomy in foreign policy, in consonance with the line upheld by most Latin American countries. (Carcar and Filmus, 2010)

Among the measures adopted, the national government repaid the debt to the International Monetary Fund in 2005, nationalized the airline Aerolineas Argentinas (Law No. 26,466 of 2008), Yacimientos Petrolíferos Fiscales (Law No. 26,741 of 2012) and the social security system (Law No. 26,425 of 2012). It also promoted the creation of new regional organizations, such as UNASUR (2008) and CELAC (2011). The objective was to have control once again of the central instruments and resources of public policy.

The global context at this time presented a more multipolar world, in which new relevant actors emerged on the international scene, such China, Russia, India and Brazil, who began to press for the modification of the structures of international organizations so as better to represent the new balances of world power. In this context, political processes emerged in Latin America that confronted the neoliberal proposals of the central countries. The governments that took office in Latin America at this time, mainly progressive and left-wing, promoted a policy that sought – with its vicissitudes – to strengthen regional integration.

Argentina redefined its perspective and foreign policy alliances, abandoning the automatic alignment with the United States that had been typical of the 1990s. The groupings promoted by the South American countries themselves were strengthened as mechanisms of South American integration that allowed the region better to position itself in the international community. Foreign policy was mainly oriented towards alliances in the region.

MERCOSUR was understood "as the expression of its own and institutionalized form of integration between the peoples of its Member States, aimed at guaranteeing economic and social development (not only free trade) in democracy" as well as a vector of independent insertion in the international system. UNASUR was consolidated as the instrument that allowed the region "to advance specific South American interests on the basis of political agreement" (Pereyra Ruy, 2012). It had gained momentum at the Meeting of Presidents of South America, held in Brasilia in 2000, in which the heads of government "agreed on the assessment that political stability, economic growth and the promotion of social justice in each of the twelve countries of South America will depend to a large extent on the expansion and deepening of cooperation and the sense of solidarity existing at the regional level and on the strengthening and expansion of the network of reciprocal interests" (Declaration of Brasilia, 1 September 2000).

As part of the policy to strengthen the region, the Community of Latin American and Caribbean States (CELAC) – without the United States and Canada – was created and launched in 2011. It is an inter-governmental mechanism of dialogue and political agreement, which for the first time brought together the thirty-three countries of Latin America and the Caribbean on a permanent basis.

New diagnosis

From 1989 to 2003, forty-seven bilateral understandings were reached between Argentina and the UK, of which seventeen dealt with the Malvinas Islands Between 2003 and 2015 there were only eight understandings, of which three dealt with aspects of the islands. For example, an exchange of notes of 3 August 2006 established the approach to unexploded ammunition found within the mined areas on the islands and a contract was made with Cranfield University to carry out tasks of the feasibility study for de-mining. But from 2003 there was a renewed focus on the substantive dispute: sovereignty. The main policy-makers of the new period understood that the policy of *rapprochement* had not been effective. As Jorge Taiana explained, (interview, 2013), "Just as we had seen that at no time had all these provisional agreements brought us closer to the sovereignty negotiating table, so we had also seen a bit of the opposite: the realization of the agreements tended to create a certain consolidation of the *status quo* and a gradual strengthening of the British position." In the same vein, Eduardo Airaldi (interview, 2013) characterized the difference between the periods in relation to the objectives of both governments:

In the government of Menem the objective was to generate a *rapprochement*; it was not that the question of sovereignty had been put aside, but that objective was not emphasized. It was considered that it was not wise to set that goal if we wanted to have a rich relationship with the United Kingdom.

After Néstor Kirchner assumed the presidency, Argentina began to review the policy of the 1990s agreements: the government stopped the fishing agreement, denounced the understanding on hydrocarbons and maintained some agreements that it considered essential. A diplomatic offensive was launched, especially regionally, to make the Malvinas part of the agenda of the new organizations.

The new approach on the part of Argentina redefined its view on the relationship with the UK and on the relationship with the islanders, upheld the importance of the legal claim, and deepened the search for support in the different international forums. It also focused its gaze on domestic politics.

The first point of the new diagnosis was that the *rapprochement* with the United Kingdom had not improved Argentina's position: "The entire period of the 1990s had a political logic that has been trivialized with the idea of *Winnie-the-Pooh*, but it is a logic that said: let us show good will and this will lead to better conditions for negotiating with the United Kingdom over the question of sovereignty. But the UK gave nothing in fifteen years. Argentine goodwill had not served to bring us closer to a situation in which one says 'well, a little more and they are going to sit down to negotiate'" (interview with Jorge Taiana, 2013).

The second point was that the legal claim was losing force: "The claim had been maintained in the Decolonization Committee, in MERCOSUR, all that was there. But to some extent it had dropped a level. There was no reason to say the claim had been lessened but the overt intensity had been lowered. The subject was almost gone from the scene" (interview with Jorge Taiana, 2013). Taiana later called it "a policy of firmness".

The Argentine government proposed to put an end to the so-called *demalvinization process*. The Argentine claim had developed, with the exception of the 1982 war, through diplomatic channels. "Demalvinization" had begun since the ending of the war. The Argentine government sought to drive a wedge between the vindication of sovereignty and any or all justification for the war. As the Argentine government understood, it was now necessary to intervene in those situations that strengthened the British position. The new view of transitional understandings did not change the meaning and importance that the decision-makers on Malvinas gave to the mechanism known as the "sovereignty umbrella". Some agreements had to be dismantled, but not the mechanism that had made them possible.

Argentina sought international support at two levels: from those countries and organizations that had expressed their support for the parties to sit down to negotiate, and from those countries that had recognized legitimate Argentine rights of sovereignty over the islands. The context in which the search for international support was developed was the deepening of the Latin American integration.

Regarding the relationship with the islanders, the perspective from 2003 onwards was not univocal. The recovery of the history of the links between the islands and the continent began to be considered a means to strengthen the Argentine position. In the recovery of this history are the social, commercial, and other cooperative ties, as well as the family stories, of the descendants of the islanders who are on the islands, but also in Río Gallegos, in Buenos Aires, in San Julián, and in Córdoba.

The recovery of family ties

Guillermo Clifton, or "Willy", is named after his grandfather, who was born in the islands. He lives in Río Gallegos and researches on agricultural production and technology. In 2004, he made contact with his family on the islands and since then has maintained a good relationship, especially with Louis Clifton, the son of his cousin, an influential person in the archipelago. "My great-grandfather came to the Malvinas in 1869, from Wales", says Willy. "He had eleven children, including my grandfather, who was born in 1898 and, after the First World War, left for the mainland since he did not have a job on the islands. The family was distributed throughout the world; one part stayed on the islands, another went to New Zealand." The identity document of his grandfather, until 1965, was the one that the metropolis had given him, which established that he was born in the Malvinas Islands but had no nationality. Then, by choice, he adopted Argentine citizenship.

During the 1960s and 1970s, the islanders often crossed to Comodoro Rivadavia, keeping in touch with the Clifton family. When the war began, the descendants of the islanders met in Río Gallegos, and sent them letters inviting them to travel to the mainland. But contact was interrupted after the war "because the islanders didn't want to know anything," Willy says.

In 1992, Willy travelled to New Zealand on a livestock scholarship, and went to visit some of his family who lived there. Every Thursday his relatives in New Zealand, met with descendants of the islands and played darts and cards, the same games that are played on the islands. They also travelled to the Malvinas every year, via Punta Arenas. His New Zealand cousins "brought him into the family".

Louis Clifton was a councillor on the islands. He has investments in ships and in oil. He has a degree in economics and is a person with influence in government decisions. When the first companies that wanted to explore for hydrocarbons arrived in the Malvinas, he was the manager. "I met Louis," Willy says. "He sent me an email saying that he was arriving in Río Gallegos and that he wanted to be with us. He also wanted to visit the grave of my grandfather, who was his uncle." They met at the hotel where Louis was staying, and they talked for two days. They went to the cemetery, had dinner one night at his house, and another at his parents' home. In these conversations, Louis commented to Willy that there are three aspects in which the islanders need Argentina. First there was health: they need Comodoro Rivadavia or other large centres that they can access relatively quickly. The second was tourism: those who have money on the islands like to make short trips. "On the islands you can feel the isolation," Louis commented to Willy. "You feel locked up, you need to get out." The islanders were also interested in receiving more tourism, because it means paying work. The third essential was education. As much as their children can study anywhere in the world, their parents would like to have them relatively close, so that they could take a plane and be with them in a short time.

Willy's other contact was with researchers, an Irishman and an Australian who were on the islands working in animal production. As the National Institute of Agricultural Technology (INTA) of Argentina has programmes for the remote sensing of sheep – radio collars that allow knowledge of their location, for which it is necessary to have a very good map with basic information – they contacted it. They crossed to the continent field and for a week met with various producers. When they returned to the islands and commented that they wanted to do a project with Argentina, the colonial administration asked them not to remain in contact.

A few years ago, Willy travelled to the United Nations Decolonization Committee as a petitioner for Argentina. He maintains contact with his cousin's son and they have seen each other in Río Gallegos and Punta Arenas. Louis has friends in the Comodoro Rivadavia area and he travels every year to visit them. "They invited me twice to the Malvinas. I did not go on either of the two occasions. Part of the family has no problem, but another part does not want to have anything to do with any Argentine. So I didn't want to have a bad time."

Development of the bilateral relationship

On 17 June 2003, Foreign Minister Rafael Bielsa met with representatives of the islands in the United Nations Decolonization Committee. He stated there that the claim to sovereignty was an "inalienable objective of the Argentine people and a State policy continued by the new government". The next important meeting was in London, on Néstor Kirchner's first international tour as president. There he raised with British Prime Minister Tony Blair, in an informal talk, off the agenda, his intention to re-negotiate the sovereignty of the islands. Blair responded on that occasion with no more than nods and smiles. The same claim reappeared during Kirchner's speech to the United Nations General Assembly, in which he urged the UK to "respond in the affirmative" to the reopening of the negotiations.

Towards the end of the year, the official confirmation by the British government that its warships had carried nuclear weapons during the 1982 conflict caused a controversy between Buenos Aires and London. The said acknowledgment signified a violation of the Treaty of Tlatelolco, which both countries had signed. Néstor Kirchner said at the time that the UK had to apologize. The response of the British Foreign Office was that it had never been in their plans to use nuclear weapons in the Latin American zone or around the islands. There were no apologies.

The Malvinas Question was again on the public agenda of both countries: Argentina demanded to sit down to negotiate, while the UK's spokesman on Latin America affairs, Bill Rammell, insisted that Tony Blair was not going to do so. At the beginning of 2004 there were more crossed swords between the two governments, this time because of the actions of the Argentine icebreaker ARA *Almirante Irizar*, which entered the area that London claims to be the islands "exclusive economic zone" to carry out fishing control tasks. Argentina argued that the icebreaker was "in Argentine jurisdictional waters" and behaving "according to maritime rules and customs".

The following year, in May 2005, the islands were incorporated as "British territory" in the text of the Constitution of the European Union, which led to a further political conflict. The Argentine government complained about this and has continued to do so on all pertinent occasions. In 2006, the national government officially petitioned the European Union to recognize "the existence of the sovereignty dispute" over the islands, in addition to requesting that "any reference to said territories by the European institutions" recognize the controversy through the use of "the double nomenclature [Malvinas/Falkland] to refer to these territories". On 1 December 2009, Argentina reiterated its protest against the Lisbon Treaty, which includes the islands as part of British territory". That month, a new Ibero-American Summit was held – all of Latin America plus Spain and Portugal – in which the member countries signed a declaration promoted by the Argentine delegation that reaffirmed Argentine sovereignty over the Islands. In January 2013, the meeting of the Euro-Latin American Parliamentary Assembly (EuroLat) was held in Santiago de Chile, where support was achieved for the reopening of bilateral negotiations. In February 2013, prominent political and cultural personalities from eighteen countries of the European Union agreed on actions to generate debate on the Malvinas and advance the possibility of achieving *rapprochement* with the inhabitants of the archipelago. Representatives included, among others, MP Jeremy Corbyn and writer Richard Gott, for the British group; the international jurist Sophie Thénon, for France; Irish Senator Terry Leyden and Theo Van Boven of the Netherlands.

At the annual session of the United Nations Special Committee for Decolonization in 2005, islanders and Argentine representatives clashed. The islanders accused the government of Néstor Kirchner of being a "bully", in addition to expressing their disbelief that "the essence of the positions towards [the Malvinas] has not changed significantly since the military dictatorship of 1982, except that the military aggression does not seem to be on your agenda". Chancellor Bielsa then stated that the islanders' comments showed "a lack of respect", denounced the UK's "unilateral acts that contradict the spirit of cooperation", rejected the inclusion of the southern archipelagos in the European Constitution, and maintained that the British celebrations for the anniversary of the Argentine surrender on the islands caused "pain and bad taste". The Committee concluded with a new pronouncement that again urged the governments of London and Buenos Aires to resume negotiations. The document was presented by Chile and had the support of Brazil (on behalf of the entire Rio Group) and Paraguay (representing the MERCOSUR countries), as well as Uruguay, Peru, Ecuador, Guatemala and Cuba. Year after year, in this way, Argentina managed to get the Committee to issue a document favourable to both countries sitting at the negotiating table. The UK continued with its position: that there would be no negotiations on the sovereignty of the islands until that was the *wish* of the islanders.

In June 2006, the Parliamentary Observatory on the Malvinas Question was created in the Argentine Chamber of Deputies, with the purpose of generating a space for theoretical reflection and political action around the dispute over the sovereignty of the islands. The Observatory was made up of a Board of Directors of fourteen members, seven representatives from different political spaces and another seven from the academic world, and chaired by the head of the Foreign Relations Commission of the Lower House. The objective was to promote the Malvinas issue not only at the national level, but also at the international level and in multilateral forums.

On 27 June 2007 Gordon Brown became Prime Minister of the United Kingdom. In the letter of congratulation that Néstor Kirchner sent him after his inauguration, he ratified the unwavering will of the Argentine government to resume the negotiation process for reacquisition of the islands. In September of the same year, the British unilateral plan to extend the so-called "exclusive economic zone" of the islands from 200 to 350 nautical miles was announced. The British Embassy in Buenos Aires admitted that the UK was considering making the representations to the UN about the continental shelf around the islands, prompting a strong response from Argentina.

In November 2008, the UK proposed a new "Constitution for the Islands", which strengthened local democracy while retaining the powers of London to protect its interests. The new "Constitution" replaced the one of 1985. As the British Deputy Minister of Foreign Relations, Gillian Merron, noted, "what does not change is the British government's global commitment with the islands as an Overseas Territory. [...] Nor does it change the right to self-determination."

The British had already modified their discursive strategy. "They maintained a constant rejection of negotiations, saying that what they accepted between 1965 and 1981 was unacceptable, including important advances such as 1974. They use the war as disqualifying the Argentine claim, reversing the argument from force: it is not about the islands that the British occupied by violence in 1833, but about a country that went to war against a defenceless population. They don't want history to be talked about anymore, and what they want to strengthen is the message about self-determination" (interview with Jorge Taiana, 2013). The perspective of "self-determination" had been used by the UK since before 1965, but it was revitalized following the war. "Instead of debating where they know they are losing, they focus on the war and the alleged violence of the Argentines, which they see as strengthening the presumed right of the islanders to be able to live in peace in the face of this threat" (interview with Jorge Taiana, 2013).

The Argentine Chancellery affirmed, through letter of protest to the British Embassy, that the new "Constitution" imposed by the UK constituted further neglect of the United Nations resolutions and "a new violation of the spirit of understandings" designed to create an "environment conducive to the resumption of sovereignty negotiations". The protest stated that the unilateral British action constituted a new and open violation of Resolution 31/49 adopted in 1976 by the United Nations General Assembly. And it continued, "The Constitution adopted by the British government refers to the principle of self-determination of the peoples, which is totally alien, and consequently inapplicable, to the sovereignty dispute."

By February 2009, Prince William, second in line to the British Crown, was posted to the islands as a Royal Air Force (RAF) rescue pilot. The Argentine Foreign Ministry pointed out that this circumstance served to highlight, once again, the continued British military presence in land and sea areas that were part of the Argentine national territory. The British had maintained a unit of more than two thousand soldiers, "an absolutely disproportionate and irrational force for the area" (interview with Jorge Taiana, 2013).

The replacement of Blair by Brown as head of the British government did not change the relationship. President Cristina Fernández de Kirchner, the leader of the Argentine government from 10 December 2007, ratified the claim of Argentine sovereignty over the Malvinas Islands during a meeting in Chile with the new British Prime Minister, who insisted on the self-determination of the islanders.

In the increasing disagreement, hydrocarbons had a prominent place. On 22 February 2010, Cristina Fernández de Kirchner denounced the UK for its installation of an oil platform in the South Atlantic. Two days later the Argentine Foreign Minister met with the UN Secretary General, Ban Ki-moon, whom he asked to intercede with the UK to refrain from carrying out more "unilateral acts" in oil exploration and to agree to negotiate sovereignty.

On the Decolonization Committee the USA continued with its neutral position, according to the spokesperson for Secretary of State Hillary Clinton, and urged dialogue. A few days later, on 1 March 2010, Cristina Fernández de Kirchner received Mrs Clinton:

We achieved a certain change in the position of the United States, which called for us to sit down and talk. The United States has always argued that it does not touch on bilateral issues, but we achieved a certain compromise. Why? Because in a set of statements obtained, we transformed the issue into a regional one. If Hillary Clinton wanted to have a more or less successful policy towards the region, she had to address the issue. That is why she came to Argentina [...] This shows that even with the United Kingdom's strategic allies, such as the United States, a small movement can be achieved if the political wills and Latin American regional agreements are brought together. (Interview with Jorge Taiana, 2013)

On 22 June 2010, Héctor Timerman, until then Argentine ambassador to the United States, took over as foreign minister from Taiana. At the United Nations, Timerman renewed the protest against the illegitimate occupation of the islands during the annual meeting of the Committee on Decolonization. He stated that the unilateral and illegal decision by British companies to explore non-renewable natural resources in the waters surrounding the islands were facts that constituted an environmental threat for the southern countries of Latin America and expressed concern, in turn, at the significant military presence that the UK had illegally established with its base in the Malvinas.

Faced with the increase in British unilateral actions, in mid-2010, the Argentine Chamber of Deputies approved a bill that led to National Law No. 26,659: Conditions for the exploration and exploitation of hydrocarbons on the Argentine Continental Shelf. The norm prohibits the extraction of oil from the continental shelf of Argentina if there is no authorization from the Ministry of Energy, enables the Executive Power to control the companies that work in the search for and exploitation of hydrocarbons in the said maritime area, and applies sanctions to companies that carry out such actions without approval of the enforcement authority designated by the Argentine State. It was intended to discourage companies from making agreements with the UK to explore for and eventually exploit oil in the disputed territory.

In 2006, the Argentine Foreign Ministry began to request that neighbouring countries not facilitate the use of ports and airports for British ships and planes bound for the Malvinas or other South Atlantic islands whose sovereignty was in dispute. In September 2010 the Uruguayan government denied entry to the port of Montevideo to a frigate of the British navy that needed to replenish food and fuel. The ship, HMS Gloucester D-96, had requested authorization to dock in the Uruguayan capital, which was rejected at the request of the Ministry of Foreign Affairs of that country, in accordance with the policy of support that the government of President José Mujica maintained for the Argentine claim of sovereignty of the South Atlantic Islands. Unlike the response given by Uruguay, in December 2010 Chile authorized one of the British warships to call at one of its ports, ignoring the UNASUR resolution in Guyana, by which the member states agreed to prevent the entry of vessels that participated in military exercises.

In October 2010, Argentina protested at British military exercises on the Islands. A month later, Argentina accused the UK in the United Nations International Maritime Organization (IMO) of carrying out, for 28 years, naval exercises in the illegitimately occupied territory of the South Atlantic without making the required notifications.

Towards the end of that the British Prime Minister, David Cameron, reiterated that the UK "was not going to negotiate the sovereignty of the islands unless the islanders consented". Timerman replied that the islanders were an "implanted" population, and that they could not be considered native. The discursive escalation continued in June 2011, when Cameron ratified the "right to self-determination". The Argentine Foreign Ministry rejected his statements and President Cristina Kirchner deprecated the British refusal to negotiate.

In December 2011, on the grounds of protecting endangered species in the South Atlantic Islands area, London confirmed that it planned to expand its military control zone of action and delimit fishing areas. The protection zone would encompass South Georgia and Sandwich, located about 1,300 kilometres southeast of the Malvinas. In response, Argentine Defence Minister Arturo Puricelli rejected the plan and demanded that the UK "agree to accept the requirements of the international community to discuss the Malvinas Question".

In the same month, José Mujica prevented the entry of fishing vessels flying the Falkland Islands flag to Uruguayan ports. The Presidents of the MERCOSUR member countries had supported Argentina's claim to sovereignty. They signed an agreement by which ships that carry the illegal flag of the islands as their insignia could not call upon the ports of the MERCOSUR member countries. It was not a blockade towards the islands.What was established are regulations that specify that every ship that goes to the islands has to request permission from Argentina.

At the beginning of 2012 a tourist boat from Chile was not authorized to stop in the Malvinas. The government of the islands argued health reasons. It was the British response to the MERCOSUR agreement. The statement from the Argentine Foreign Ministry said that the ship had complied with health protocols and hoped that the measure was based on objective reasons and not the "umpteenth hostile act directed at tourists of various nationalities, as well as against Argentine citizens who have the desire and the aspiration to know the Malvinas Islands".

The pronouncements of British officials on the Malvinas increased in intensity after Argentina obtained the support of the CELAC countries (excluding the United States and Canada) and of MERCOSUR and Chile. Cameron accused Argentina of being "colonialist", and reaffirmed again that as long as the islanders want to remain British, they should be able to be so. With the same argument of the right to self-determination, the English Foreign Secretary, William Hague, reiterated that the Falklanders had "the right to determine their own future and develop its own community and economy".

Towards the end of January 2012, Alicia Castro was appointed Argentine Ambassador to the United Kingdom. The position had been vacant for three years. The Foreign Ministry stated: "Since the arrival of Ambassador Alicia Castro in March 2012, the accent has been placed on conveying to British public opinion the message that Argentina seeks dialogue with the United Kingdom, in accordance with repeated calls from the United Nations (41 resolutions that urge the governments of Argentina and the United Kingdom to resume negotiations to peacefully and definitively resolve the sovereignty dispute). Along with this message we have tried to make it clear that our country does not constitute a military threat to the United Kingdom (as some British media claim) since our Constitution and the unanimous decision of Argentine society indicate that the only way to resolve the controversy is through peaceful means."

On the last day of that month, the British Ministry of defence announced that at the end of March the vessel HMS Dauntless, armed with high-tech anti-aircraft missiles, heliports and carrying 60 Marines, would depart for the South Atlantic. They claimed that the decision was a "routine deployment", although the Royal Navy maintained that it would cause "Argentina to pause and reflect" on its claim to sovereignty. The Argentine response was a new formal presentation on 10 February before the President of the United Nations Security Council, Kodjo Menan, noting that "once again, the Argentine Republic is obliged to alert the international community, through the main organs of the United Nations, on the increasing British militarization of the Malvinas Islands". The following day, the Argentine Foreign Minister approved the offer of mediation by the President of the United Nations General Assembly,

Nassir Abdulaziz Al-Nasser.

On 25 February 2012, all the members of the Foreign Relations Commissions of the Chamber of Deputies and the Chamber of Senators of the Congress of the Argentine Nation signed the Declaration of Ushuaia, "which ratifies Argentine sovereignty over the Malvinas Islands, appreciates the solidarity of the Latin American countries and rejects the process of militarization of the islands by the United Kingdom". As stated by the president of the Senate Foreign Relations Committee, Daniel Filmus, the declaration "reaffirms the wish for dialogue and peace of the Argentine Republic with respect to the Malvinas Islands in a sustained effort to recover the full exercise of sovereignty. This declaration is not from a government or from a particular historical moment: the Malvinas Question is a permanent question for this Congress and for all the political forces of Argentina".

A few days later, the Argentine government proposed to reduce imports from the UK. The Minister of Industry, Débora Giorgi, communicated with the heads of more than twenty national and multinational firms that acquired British goods and had increased the volume of their purchases in 2011. In response, the UK asked the European Union to support its repudiation of the trade sanctions Argentina intended to carry out. The national government, through the Chancellery, was "pleased" that the British "have finally resorted to a forum to seek a diplomatic solution to the Malvinas Question".

Towards the end of the year, there was a new exchange between Cristina Kirchner and David Cameron. After the open letter with which the President urged him to put an end to colonialism and return the archipelago, the Prime Minister replied through the British television channel BBC that he would fight to preserve the islands, and that he had one of the five largest defence forces in the world.

In February 2013, the British government launched a new initiative: it promoted a "referendum" for the inhabitants of the islands to express their willingness or not to remain British. The vote was held on 10 and 11 March. Its foreseeable result was that 99.8% of the inhabitants were in favour of continuing to be part of the "British overseas territory". Cameron said that Argentina "should take careful note of this result". The Argentine ambassador in London, Alicia Castro, affirmed that the consultation was a "media manoeuvre" and argued that "it was a referendum organized by the British for the British, in order for them to say that the territory has to be British".

The British government did not get the same response when seeking international support. The State Department of the United States, headed by John Kerry, did not change its position after the referendum. For the European Commission, the referendum in the Malvinas was "an internal issue". The spokesman for the European Union, Olivier Bailly, refused to comment on the matter. "They are British to the core," declared the British Prime Minister, while from Puerto Argentino one of the eight members of the so-called "Legislative Assembly" of the islands, Gavin Short, warned the Argentine government that the inhabitants of the islands have "absolutely no desire to be run by the Buenos Aires government".

The Argentine Embassy responded to the UK's "referendum" with a document of March 2013 entitled "The United Nations, the Malvinas Question and the principle of self-determination":

a) It has no effect from the point of view of international law.

b) In no way alters the essence of the Question of the Malvinas Islands and its foreseeable outcome does not put an end to the dispute.

c) Only British citizens participate in the elections held on the islands and only British citizens participated in the referendum.

d) Unlike other cases of decolonization, this referendum was not called for by the United Nations, nor does it have its approval or supervision.

e) The result will not end the dispute. The islands will continue to be a territory subject to decolonization.

f) The countries of the region have rejected the holding of the referendum through declarations by UNASUR and MERCOSUR.

Towards the end of 2013, the Argentine government ordered the creation of the Secretariat for Affairs Relating to the Malvinas Islands, South Georgia and the South Sandwich Islands and the Surrounding Maritime Spaces in the South Atlantic, within the framework of the Ministry of Foreign Affairs. The decision to elevate the area with thematic competence to Secretariat level was "a reaffirmation of the deep commitment to a cause that is not only of the Argentines but also of all the peoples that fight for the end of the colonialism and respect for the territorial integrity of independent nations" (Decree 2.251/2013). Daniel Filmus, until then senator and president of the Foreign Relations Committee of the Upper House, assumed the direction of the new Secretariat on 6 January 2014. The objective was the implementation of strategies and actions, from the point of view of foreign policy in relations with all countries, for the better defence of Argentine rights and interests in the Malvinas Question. Its creation reaffirmed the importance of the issue for the national government, expanded its resources and promoted its role to the highest level of the structure of the Argentine Foreign Ministry. Its objectives include the execution of bilateral actions, assistance to the Minister of Foreign Affairs in bilateral negotiations, the design of strategies and the coordination of actions with all countries to defend Argentine rights and interests, as well as the dissemination of Argentine rights throughout the world.

The Secretariat continued to strengthen the work carried out by the General Directorate of the Malvinas and South Atlantic Islands, through diplomatic channels, which had managed to position the Malvinas Question as a regional cause, in addition to attracting the support of countries from other regions through the pronouncement of multiple forums and international organizations. In addition to the declarations in support of the legitimate rights in the sovereignty dispute issued by MERCOSUR, UNASUR, ALBA, CELAC and the 54 African countries, were added the pronouncements in favour of the resumption of sovereignty negotiations of the Summits of South American and Arab Countries (ASPA) and the Group of 77 plus China, as well as that of the Latin American Energy Organization.

Likewise, a legal offensive was launched, through the enactment of a law amending Law No. 26,915, which established criminal penalties for companies and leaders engaged in the illegal exploration and exploitation of hydrocarbons on the Argentine continental shelf. The aim of the legislation was to protect renewable and non-renewable natural resources in the South Atlantic against illegitimate unilateral activities carried out by the UK. The Secretariat also promoted the development of research projects in universities, the production of short films about the Malvinas, the dissemination of historical material, researcher meetings, as well as participation in forums in the country and abroad.

In April 2014, the UK conducted further missile tests on the islands. The Argentine government considered the exercise a new provocation, part of the increasing militarization of the South Atlantic, and presented a protest note to the UK.

On 6 June 2014, the Argentine government created the Museum of Malvinas and Islas del Atlántico Sur, with the aim of disseminating, communicating, exhibiting and raising awareness about the sovereignty rights of Argentina over the islands, as well as promoting the claim of the Malvinas cause as an Argentine, Latin American and universal cause Decree 809/2014).

Provisional agreements

The mechanism of the "sovereignty umbrella" continued in force, as it was considered an ideal mechanism to arrive at new understandings that could be beneficial.

Communications

The communications agreement referred mainly to air access and services and to confidence-building measures, such as establishing the Monument to the Fallen.

As for air services, the understanding referred to regular flights between the islands and the mainland, not to charter flights. One of the first measures of the Argentine government was to intervene in it. Charter flights highlighted the tension between two conceptions of law, that of civil law and that of public international law, in which custom is the source of law. To the extent that all charter flights were authorized "by exception" every time they were requested, the British were, in effect, building a new right. In November 2003 the Argentine government suspended charter flights between the continent and the islands, and reported that it would not continue to authorize them as long as they did not depart from Argentine territory. In this regard, Argentina proposed that the UK reach a provisional understanding to expand regular flights by establishing new direct air services between continental Argentina and the islands, operated by an Argentine company. The British response was that an agreement on charter flights had to be negotiated first, which was not accepted since the priority for Argentina was regular flights. From then on, it stopped authorizing charter flights between third countries and the islands operated by third-party companies. This measure did not apply to the regular flights covered by the Joint Declaration of 14 July 1999, nor to the private ones covered by the agreement of 23 February 2001, nor to medical evacuations or other emergencies.

The second intervention on the issue of flights was linked to the stopovers of ships and military aeroplanes. There was an agreement whereby neither aeroplanes nor warships refuelled in the ports of neighbouring countries, but in practice they asked for an exception permit and it was granted. It was then decided to demand that the neighbouring countries comply with this agreement, as receiving warships or planes that travelled with people and weapons was a way of contributing to the British occupation military effort.

A new negotiation attempt was made in March 2012. The Argentine ambassador to the United Kingdom, Alicia Castro, presented a note to the British Minister of State Jeremy Browne, with an Argentine proposal to up the weekly flights of Aerolineas Argentinas to three with departures from Jorge Newbery Airport. The island representatives were quick to disagree with the Argentine proposal. "I am quite surprised at the proposal when, at the same time, we are not allowed to charter flights using Argentine airspace," said Sharon Halford, one of the eight members of the Legislative Assembly of the archipelago.

The Monument to the Argentine Fallen in the Malvinas Islands, agreed in 1999, was built between February and April 2004. In March 2005, the directors of the Commission of Relatives of the Fallen made a visit to the Islands to verify the completion of the work, but its inauguration by the British side was delayed. Four years later, after the intervention of the national government, in October 2009 the monument was inaugurated, in a formal ceremony in the Darwin cemetery.

Fishing resources
Regarding the Joint Declaration on the Conservation of Fishery Resources of 28 November 1990, the Argentine perspective that the agreements were provisional to generate conditions to discuss the sovereignty claim was interpreted by the UK as proof that it was possible to coexist perfectly without the claim. In 2005, the government sent fifteen protest notes to the UK criticising its "illegitimate unilateral acts" and challenging decisions related to the exploitation of fishing and oil exploration. In that year, the last two meetings of the South Atlantic Fisheries Commission (CPAS) were held. After the July meeting of the Commission, a warning was made about unilateral British measures aimed at providing long-term fisheries resources. The Argentine government proposed, for the next meeting, a draft agenda aimed at analyzing the mandate of the Commission and to what extent it was affected by these measures. The last meeting was held on 6 December 2005, without UK agreement to adopt the agenda proposed by Argentina. Since then the Commission has not met and all the cooperation mechanisms provided for in the Joint Declaration have been suspended.

In July 2006 there was a complaint from the Chancellery about a new fishing law which extended the fishing licenses granted by the UK to 25 years, which described it as an "illicit and unilateral long-term provision" in maritime spaces under sovereignty dispute. The unilateral British provision was contrary to Resolution 31/49 of the United Nations General Assembly, which urged the two parties to the dispute to refrain from adopting unilateral modifications in the disputed area. This increase in unilateral actions led on 20 June 2008 to the Argentine government promulgating Law No. 26,386, modifying the Federal

Fishing Regime (Law No. 24,922) empowering it to act in relation to companies that exploit fishing resources in the Argentine exclusive economic zone without authorization.

Hydrocarbons

On 27 March 2007, the Argentine government communicated to the United Kingdom its decision to terminate the Joint Declaration of Cooperation on Offshore Activities in the Southwest Atlantic, signed in 1995. The cancellation of the agreement sought to remove legitimacy from the UK, which used the agreement as "an instrument by which the United Kingdom tried to justify its illegitimate and repeated unilateral action, exploring areas of the Argentine continental shelf with the purpose of exploiting resources that belong to the Argentines" (interview with Jorge Taiana, 2013). London called the Argentine decision "regrettable" and argued that it would not help Argentina in its claim for the sovereignty of the islands. Two days after suspending the understanding, Argentina prohibited oil companies that operate or have operated in the islands to carry out work in the national territory.

Hydrocarbons returned to the fore in April 2008, when the Chancellery filed a complaint with the British government over the granting of licences for the exploration and exploitation of oil fields. According to the statement issued by the Argentine Foreign Ministry, "The energetic protest [...] responds to the firm and constant policy of the government in the face of the succession of British unilateral actions that, among other reasons, led Argentina to terminate the cooperation." The government then presented a formal complaint to the UK for the "illegitimate opening of the licensing round". In February 2010, hydrocarbon drilling activities began in the north of the islands, in areas of the continental shelf subject to sovereignty dispute. The Argentine government presented a new protest note to the UK, rejecting its claim to authorize hydrocarbon exploration activities in the areas surrounding the islands by means of the Ocean Guardian platform. In response, the UK made it known that its diplomacy was on "alert because it handles the hypothesis that Argentina may try to block the arrival to the islands of the oil platform, which is being transferred by sea from Scotland".

As a measure intended to discourage the exploitation of natural resources, the Argentine government issued Decree No. 256/2010, which applies to the movement of ships and naval devices between continental ports and those of the disputed islands (its Rules of Application were published on 26 April 2010). The decree established that "any vessel that intends to transit between ports located in the Argentine mainland and in the Malvinas, South Georgia and South Sandwich Islands must request prior authorization" and created, within the scope of the Chief of Cabinet of Ministers, the Permanent Commission for the Evaluation of Regulations. The provision was in line with Resolution No. 407/07, which established sanctions for those who maintained a beneficial relationship with those involved in activities contrary to international law, derived from the illegal occupation of the islands.

Towards the end of February, the British oil company Desire Petroleum began its oil exploration operations off the islands. The platform arrived at the first of the wells, located 400 kilometres from Santa Cruz. The exclusion zone, formed 500 metres around the Ocean Guardian platform, was monitored by warships. The first of the strategic points on which the work began was 200 kilometres north of the islands and 300 kilometres from the capital of the island. The oil rig was accompanied by Danish-flagged Maersk Traveler vessels, the Ahts Maersk Pacer logistics vessel and the Bahamian-flagged PSV Toisa Invincible. The British press claimed that the islands potentially contained some 60 billion barrels of crude. At the end of March, Desire revealed that in the first of the wells explored the oil reserves were of poor quality and were at great depth, which made the operation unviable. The company's shares on the stock market were reduced to half their value. In the second find, the company announced a new discovery in the northern basin of the Islands, although it had yet to be determined whether it was commercially exploitable. Both firms, associated with Falkland Oil & Gas, had begun a drilling project in the waters adjacent to the islands in February 2009. The announcements came three months after London had unilaterally granted exploration permits in the north of the islands, in areas under sovereignty dispute.

In October 2010, the Argentine government took legal action against the company Fugro NV, which had started oil exploration in the Malvinas with only British permission. In February 2011, the Argentine government prevented a consignment of seamless pipes, produced by the Techint corporation, from being shipped on the foreign-flagged ship Thor Leader, which came from the islands. The following day, the Undersecretary of Ports and Inland Waterways of the Ministry of Planning formalized the prohibition of the Thor Leader vessel from carrying out any operation in Argentine ports, until it complied with existing regulations, established by provision No. 108 of the Undersecretariat of Ports and Inland Waterways. On 16 March 2011, Law 26,659 was enacted, which created conditions for the exploration and exploitation of hydrocarbons in the Argentine Continental Shelf and provided sanctions of between five and twenty years of disqualification for non-compliance.

In May 2010, the British company Rockhopper Explorations announced that it had discovered oil in the northern basin of the Islands, in the Sea Lion exploration block, with an estimated potential of 242 million barrels. In October Rockhopper indicated that the reserve would be thick and of high quality and that it would be commercially viable. In November 2011, a new statement from the Rockhopper referred to a further discovery, in a well 2,696 metres deep, and that its expectations of quantity and quality was high.

In a further escalation, in January 2012, Falkland Oil & Gas Limited announced that it obtained 75 million US dollars for new drilling. Towards March, the Argentine government announced that it would carry out administrative, civil and criminal prosecutions against the oil, logistics and financial companies that had participated in the "illegitimate exploration activities" on the maritime area of the Malvinas Islands, "ignoring Argentine legislation and resolutions of the United Nations". In response, the British Foreign Office called the Argentine government's decision "illegal, improper and totally counterproductive". The statement expressed the belief that the exploration of hydrocarbons on the islands was a legitimate commercial activity, that the British government supported the right of the inhabitants of the islands to develop their own oil resources for their own economic benefit, and that such a right was integral to their self-determination. Five administrative proceedings were then initiated before the Federal Administration of Public Revenues (AFIP), after which the Argentine Energy company (ENARSA) presented itself as an injured party, as the company had been awarded the offshore oil areas of the continent. The Ministry of Energy criticised the companies Rockhopper Exploration, Desire Petroleum, Argos Resources, Falkland Oil & Gas Limited and Borders & Southern Petroleum. The Chancellery reported that the "clandestine" status of the companies and the implementation of legal actions was communicated to the host countries of the oil companies, the London Stock Exchange Regulatory Body, the British Treasury, the International Organization of Securities Commissions and the New York Stock Exchange. One of the responses received was a note from the British Petroleum company on April 10, 2012, which reported that it "does not participate in hydrocarbon exploration activities in the region, nor does it have plans to do so in the future". Other companies continued nevertheless with the exploration of natural resources.

In turn, a working group was established made up of the Attorney

General's Office and the National Treasury, the Federal Administration of Public Revenues (AFIP) and the Ministry of Energy, in order to develop a legal strategy, within the framework of administrative, civil and criminal filings against oil, logistics and financial companies involved in hydrocarbon exploration over the maritime area of the Malvinas Islands.

In reaction to British advances, in December 2013 the Argentine Congress enacted Law No. 26,915, which amended Articles 7 to 11 of Law No. 26,659 on exploration and exploitation of hydrocarbons. The objective of the modifications was to establish criminal sanctions for companies and leaders who engage in the illegal exploration and exploitation of hydrocarbons on the Argentine continental shelf.

On 16 December 2013, the British Foreign Office delivered to the Argentine Chargé d'Affaires in London a note rejecting the amendments and accused Argentina of wanting to "strangle" the economy of the archipelago. The particularity of the note is that "the British Government protests against legislation that only speaks of the Argentine continental shelf and that does not expressly mention the disputed territories". In response, the Argentine government's note stressed that the MERCO-SUR heads of state "have recognized the right of Argentina to adopt legal actions implemented within the scope of its legislation, against unauthorized exploration and exploitation of hydrocarbons. in the controversial area".

Continental shelf

After an exchange of information between Argentina and the United Kingdom, regarding preparatory activities for their presentations before the Commission on the Limits of the Continental Shelf, two meetings were held in Buenos Aires, in June 2001 and in December 2004. Argentina endorsed its sovereign rights "over a vast territory of 1,782,645km² of Argentine continental shelf that extends beyond its exclusive economic zone and throughout the natural extension of its continental territory, the Islands of the South Atlantic and the Argentine Antarctic sector, additional to 4,799,732 km2, up to 200 miles". The Commission did not examine the submissions made by Argentina and the United Kingdom by virtue of the provisions of Annex I of the Commission's Regulations, which establishes that it does not consider or qualify submissions referring to areas under sovereignty dispute.

The Declaration on the Question of the Malvinas Islands of UNASUR, issued on May 4, 2010 also rejects the exploration activities of non-renewable natural resources of the Argentine continental shelf carried out by the United Kingdom, in open opposition to the provisions of

Resolution 31/49 of the United Nations.

On 26 November 2010, the member countries of UNASUR undertook to adopt all measures required to prevent ships flying the illegal flag of the Falkland Islands from entering their ports, and to inform the Argentine government about those ships with cargo destined for illegal hydrocarbon and/or mining activities on the Argentine continental shelf.

International support

The Argentine government extended its search for international support in order to give greater profundity to its claim. The search was oriented both towards multilateral organizations and to the level of bilateral relations and the supporters constitute an impressively international list, albeit one too lengthy to detail here. Six Nobel Peace Laureates also expressed their support in 2012, in a letter signed by Adolfo Pérez Esquivel, Desmond Tutu, Rigoberta Menchú, Mairead Maguire, Jody Williams and Shirin Ebadi: "We request that the British government review its position of not talking (on sovereignty) and we reiterate our request to comply with United Nations resolutions."

A significant achievement of the period was the support of the Community of Latin American and Caribbean States (CELAC). "The most important diplomatic triumph we had in these years was getting CELAC – which includes the Caribbean countries, even those whose Head of State is the Queen of England – to accept the Rio Group standard, which recognized the sovereign rights of Argentina (interview with Jorge Taiana (2013) Thus, Mexico's declaration of February 2010 was taken up in the Special Communiqué on the Malvinas Islands, within the framework of CELAC in December 2011. At the third Summit of Heads of State and Government of CELAC in 2015, support for Argentina was ratified, through a special statement that expressed the "strongest support for the legitimate rights of the Argentine Republic in the sovereignty dispute".

Continuities

There are not only differences between the various periods surveyed in this study, but also continuities. The first great continuity is that Argentina has never ceased to claim its legitimate sovereign rights over the Islands. The permanent position of Argentina has been that the sovereignty dispute involves only two States. On the contrary, the British have not been consistent in their treatment of the colonies under their rule.

Another significantly important continuity has been the value given to the "sovereignty umbrella" as a mechanism that frames the relationship with the UK. The mechanism allows that the negotiations or agreements on practical matters that are carried out do not imply changes in the claims to sovereignty. This permits Argentina to negotiate new understandings that are considered of interest.

The Malvinas throughout these decades has remained a strategic location for the United Kingdom, because of the military base they have there and because of the natural resources present in the area, hydrocarbons and a maritime platform with significant fishing resources. It is also considered important as a "possible gate" to Antarctica, one of the most important freshwater reserves in the world.

The analysis leaves some questions open. In particular, there are still classified files on the Malvinas Question, which, when declassified, will shed light on the different periods in question. Likewise, one might carry out a comparative study that allows for the contrasting of both perspectives: what were the differing inflections of the various British governments from 1982 onwards, for example?

The reorientation of Argentine foreign policy towards Latin America, in the context of a multipolar world in which the importance of the United States is accompanied by the emergence of new actors, has strengthened Argentina's position before the international community. The region as a whole will be consolidated if it manages to deepen the regional integration processes.

As long as the region demands and contributes to the resumption of negotiations, it will continue to increase the substance of the claim and favour its resolution. The British policy of exploration and exploitation of natural resources – renewable and non-renewable – in the South Atlantic, as well as the militarization of the islands, are a source of alarm for all the countries of Latin America. The resumption of the sovereignty negotiations is one way of contributing to the peace efforts in the region.

The Argentine rejection of repeated unilateral British actions – in hydrocarbons, in fisheries resources, in the militarization of the region, among others – has shown the international community that the UK continues to ignore the United Nations resolutions.

The resolution of the dispute will also depend on whether the country and the region continue to grow and develop. The long-term progress of the country and the region is, at least, as important as the development of a coherent policy which convinces the different countries of the legitimacy of the Argentine claim.

The continuity of the pendulum

> We have to explore dialogue and collaboration with the United Kingdom beyond Malvinas [...] The Islands are no longer the dominant issue in the relationship between Argentina and the United Kingdom and should not divert attention from the most important bilateral priorities like trade and investment.
>
> Susana Malcorra, former Foreign Minister of Argentina, 2016

What has happened since my book *Malvinas: soberanía y vida cotidiana* was published in 2015?

On 10 December of that year, Mauricio Macri assumed the Argentine presidency, establish a new orientation in foreign policy. The UK was heading towards Brexit, its eventual self-removal from the European Union. In Latin America there was a shift to the right, with the establishment of various conservative governments in the region (Erlich, 2019). Under the Macri presidency, Argentina tried to re-triangulate its relations with Europe and the USA in a context in which the latter, after the presidential inauguration of Donald Trump, was increasingly prone to closing its borders and advancing a protectionist policy. While protectionism in these countries advanced, in Argentina the new government insisted on opening up imports and entering into free trade agreements.

As for Malvinas, this meant once again lowering the manifest intensity of the Argentine claim. Since the beginning of the Macri government, the sovereignty of the Malvinas Islands has ceased to be part of the political agenda proposed by Argentina. Macri was the first democratically elected president since 1983 who did not include the

Malvinas Question in his presidential inauguration speech.

As part of this repositioning, in March 2016, the new government removed the rank of the Secretariat for Affairs Relating to the Malvinas Islands of the Ministry of Foreign Affairs, which had been created in 2013. On 16 May 2016, the then Foreign Minister Susana Malcorra said in an interview with the *The Financial Times* that the Malvinas were no longer "the main issue of the relationship with Great Britain".

The policy of the recent period is revealed in the joint communiqué signed between the two countries on 13 September 2016, which essentially expresses British demands, while making none of the historic Argentine demands. No mention is made of the sovereignty dispute, United Nations Resolution 2065 (XX) or the violation of Resolution 31/49 that prohibits unilateral actions. Nor is anything said about the illegal existence of a British military base in the South Atlantic peace zone (Filmus and Erlich, 2017).

Paradoxically, concessions to British demands were made in the context of Brexit and the consequent international difficulties faced by the UK. The UK Foreign Secretary between 2010 and 2014, William Hague, warned two weeks before the Brexit referendum, "the leave vote would put the sovereignty of the Falklands at risk". At the same time, Jeremy Corbyn, then leader of the British Labour Party, argued that bilateral dialogue with Argentina was the only alternative solution to the sovereignty dispute.

Nothing changed the government approach. Macri's government restarted a policy that was close to the one promoted during the 1990s, despite being aware of the British unilateral acts during the previous decades and the – already known – results of the 1990s policies.

One month after the joint communiqué of September 2016, which included a section on "International security and defence" in which it was agreed that "closer cooperation is required to face threats to international peace and security", the British held further military exercises in the islands. In continuity with British demands, on 20 November 2019 – National Sovereignty Day in Argentina, and a few days before the end of the presidential mandate – the second air service to the Islands became effective: the flight São Paulo-Córdoba-Falkland/Malvinas Islands was not operated by the national flag airline, Aerolíneas Argentinas, nor did it complete its journey in the Argentine national territory.

The only advance that it is possible to discern in this recent period is the continuity given to the humanitarian mission for the exhumation and identification of the 123 bodies found in the Darwin Cemetery. The initiative has been promoted by various organizations of ex-combatants in the Malvinas and undertaken since 2012, under the presidency of Cristina Fernández de Kirchner, together with the Argentine Forensic Anthropology Team (EAAF), who requested the collaboration of the International Red Cross.

Malvinas, State policy

> We reaffirm our strongest commitment to compliance with the first transitory clause of the National Constitution, and we will work tirelessly to enhance the legitimate and inalienable claim for sovereignty over the Malvinas, South Georgia and South Sandwich Islands and the corresponding maritime and insular spaces. We will do so knowing that the peoples of Latin America and the world are with us and convinced that the only possible path is that of peace and diplomacy.
>
> Alberto Fernández, presidential inauguration speech, 10 December 2019

As of 10 December 2019, with the assumption of power of Alberto Fernández as President of the Nation, a new stage of foreign policy began: Malvinas once again became a central thrust of Argentine foreign policy. Cristina Fernández de Kirchner (President from 2007 to 2015) is now vice-president. The decision of the executive power is once again to promote, in accordance with the First Transitory Clause of the National Constitution, the Malvinas Question as a State policy.

We can thus see that policy towards Malvinas has been pendular since the end of the war in 1982, and that this has been counter-productive: the lack of a sustained medium and long-term policy on the Malvinas has been fruitless with respect to the Argentine claim. One of the objectives proposed by the new government has focused on breaking this dual logic, this pendular movement. In December 2019, the government of Alberto Fernández created the Secretariat of the Malvinas, Antarctica and South Atlantic in the Ministry of Foreign Affairs, International Trade and Worship of the Nation under the direction of Daniel Filmus. Among its functions, the Secretariat has under its purview "all matters relating to the Malvinas Islands, South Georgia, South Sandwich and the surrounding maritime spaces in the South Atlantic. It designs strategies and coordinates actions at the bilateral and multilateral level for the better defence of Argentine rights and interests, while proposing courses of action for the dissemination of those rights and interests. It also oversees the policies and actions carried out by the Advisory Council on issues related to the South Atlantic. It is also in charge of planning and directing Antarctic policy and executes Argentine Antarctic activity, along with the discharge of the corresponding international commitments."

The President had already announced in his inauguration speech and at the beginning of the Parliamentary sessions the introduction of three bills to strengthen Argentine territorial sovereignty, which were later turned into laws by the National Congress, two of them unanimously, and one with the support of practically the entire political spectrum. Among the first two laws approved, Law No. 27558/2020 created the National Council for Matters Relating to the Malvinas Islands, South Georgia, South Sandwich and the Corresponding Maritime and Insular Spaces, within the scope of the Presidency of the Nation. Its functions include "contributing to growth of the political and social consensus necessary to design and implement State policies that aim to effect the full exercise of sovereignty, [... to] collaborate in the elaboration of the support of the Argentine position in the sovereignty dispute in its geographical, environmental, historical, legal and political aspects, [...to] propose and carry out teaching and research activities that provide knowledge to the Argentine people about the justice of the claim to the full exercise of sovereignty, [...to] carry out actions designed to collaborate in the dissemination and promotion of Argentine rights over the Malvinas Islands, South Georgia, South Sandwich and the Corresponding Maritime and Insular Spaces, at the regional and global level [... and] propose strategies that contribute to the permanent recognition of the Ex-Combatants of Malvinas and those killed in combat and their families."

Law No. 27757/2020 established the demarcation of the outer limit of the Argentine continental shelf, increasing legal security for the granting of concessions for the exploration of natural resources, based on the approval of the presentation presented by Argentina in 2009 before United Nations, whose Boundaries Commission validated the annexation of more than 1.7 million square kilometres to the national continental shelf."

Law No. 27564/2020, established a modification of the Federal Fisheries Regime (Law No. 24,922) promoting the sanctions regime against illegal fishing by foreign vessels in the Malvinas area.

The three laws strengthened the position of the Malvinas Question within State policy. It is still too early to judge if the policies promoted under the current government might result in success. What remains strong in the position of Argentina – and what is different from other colonial cases – is that Argentina has still not surrendered its claim while the UK has disregarded international law and the many resolutions of the international community. The analysis of the long history of the Malvinas Question shows that, despite the UK maintaining that the matter is closed, it is anything but, not only for Argentina but also for the United Nations and the international community.

It is crucial that the pendulum movement be brought to a halt; at that very point when the mid- and long-term agendas that govern Argentine State policy might coincide, when, indeed, the "Malvinas Question" is no longer a question. The first aim for the country is that Argentina and the United Kingdom sit down again – as they did before 1982 – to negotiate sovereignty over the Malvinas, in accordance with both the United Nations mandates and International Law. A second concomitant aim is to put an end, already well into the twenty-first century, to such an anachronistic case of colonialism.

Bibliography

Books and articles

Airaldi, Eduardo. "La cuestión de las Islas Malvinas en la diplomacia multilateral", n.d., available from https://www.cancilleria.gob.ar/userfiles/ut/07-eduardo_airaldi.pdf.

Argüello, Jorge. "Naciones Unidas: Cuestión Malvinas, cuestión pendiente", s.f.

Basualdo, Eduardo M. "La reestructuración de la economía argentina durante las últimas décadas de la sustitución de importaciones a la valorización financiera", in Basualdo, Eduardo and Enrique Arceo (eds.), *Neoliberalismo y sectores dominantes: Tendencias globales y experiencias nacionales*. Buenos Aires: CLACSO, Consejo Latinoamericano de Ciencias Sociales, 2006.

Beck, P. *The Falkland Islands as an International Problem*. London: Routledge, 1988.

Bernal, Federico. "Malvinas: 'La Arabia Más Austral Del Mundo'", *Le Monde Diplomatique*, n°118 (April 2009).

Blumer, Herbert. *Symbolic Interactionism: Perspective and Method*. New Jersey: Prentice Hall, 1969.

Bobbio, Norberto; Nicola Matteucci and Gianfranco Pasquino. *Diccionario de política*. México City: Siglo XXI, 1991.

Bologna, Alfredo Bruno. "La Incidencia del Conflicto de Malvinas en la Política Exterior Argentina", in *La Política Exterior Argentina 1994/1997*. Centro de Estudios en Relaciones Internacionales de Rosario (C.E.R.I.), 1998.

Calvert, P. *The Falklands Crisis: The Rights and Wrongs*. London: Francis Pinter, 1982.

Cámpora, Mario. "Malvinas y el petróleo", en *Década de Encuentro: Argentina y Gran Bretaña 1989-1999*. Buenos Aires: Nuevo hacer, 2000.

Carcar, Fabiola and Daniel Filmus, "Educación y trabajo en América Latina y Argentina en las últimas dos décadas", in Daniel Filmus (comp.), *Crisis, transformación y crecimiento: América Latina y Argentina (2000-2007)*. Buenos Aires: EUDEBA, 2010.

Cavallo, Domingo Felipe. "La inserción de la Argentina en el Primer Mundo – 1989-1991", in Silvia Ruth Jalabé (comp.), *La Política Exterior Argentina y sus protagonistas 1880-1995*. Buenos Aires: Nuevo hacer, 1996.

Cimadamore, Alberto. "Gobernabilidad y niveles de análisis en el proceso de integración del MERCOSUR" in Gerónimo De Sierra and Manuel Bernales Alvarado (ed.s), *Democracia, Gobernanza y Desarrollo en el MERCOSUR*. 2004.

Cisneros, Andrés and Escudé, Carlos. *Historia general de las relaciones exteriores de la República Argentina, Vol. XII: La diplomacia de Malvinas, 1945-1989*. Buenos Aires: Grupo Editor Latinoamericano, 2000.

Cisneros, Andrés. "Antártida y Malvinas", in Andrés Cisneros (ed.), *Apuntes para una política exterior post kirchnerista*. Buenos Aires: Editorial Planeta, 2014.

Colacrai de Trevisán, Miriam. "Perspectivas Teóricas en la Bibliografía de Política Exterior Argentina" in Roberto Russell (comp.), *Enfoques Teóricos y Metodológicos para el Estudio de la Política Exterior*. Buenos Aires: GEL, 1992.

Costa Méndez, N. *Malvinas: Ésta es la historia*, Buenos Aires: Editorial Sudamericana, 1993.

Del Carril, Bonifacio. *La Cuestión de las Malvinas: El Futuro de las Malvinas*. Buenos Aires: Emecé, s.f.

Di Tella, Guido. "Política exterior argentina: actualidad y perspectivas – 1991-1995", en Silvia Ruth Jalabé (comp.), *La Política Exterior Argentina y sus protagonistas 1880-1995*. Buenos Aires: Nuevo hacer Grupo Editor Latinoamericano, 1996.

Ellerby, C. "The Role of the Falkland Lobby, 1968-1990", in A. Danchev (ed.), *International Perspectives on the Falklands Conflict*. New York: Palgrave Macmillan, 1982.

Erlich, Uriel. "Relecturas de Malvinas y la política exterior argentina (1989-2019)", *Revista Tensões Mundiais*, v. 14 n. 27, pp. 227-251, 2019.

Erlich, Uriel. *Malvinas: soberanía y vida cotidiana*, Villa María: Eduvim, 2015.

Escudé, Carlos. *El Realismo Periférico: Fundamentos para la Nueva Política Exterior Argentina*, Buenos Aires: Planeta, 1992.

Filmus, Daniel and Uriel Erlich, *Claudicación Macrista, Revista Maíz*, ed. especial Malvinas, pp. 10-13, 2017.

Filmus, Daniel. "The Politics of Remembering and Forgetting in the Argentine Education System", in Cristina Demaria (ed.), *Post-Conflict Cultures: a Reader*. London: Critical, Cultural and Communications Press, 2020, 494-511.

Franks, O.S., *et al. Falkland Islands Review: Report of a Committee of Privy Counsellors*. London: HMSO.

Freedman, Lawrence. *The Official History of the Falklands Campaign*.

London: Routledge, 2005.

García del Solar, Lucio. "Normalización de las relaciones entre la Argentina y el Reino Unido. Acuerdos de Madrid de 1989/1990. Antecedentes y análisis", in Silvia Ruth Jalabé (comp.), *Década de Encuentro: Argentina y Gran Bretaña 1989-1999*. Buenos Aires: Nuevo Hacer, 2000.

García Moritán, Roberto: "El Petróleo de Malvinas", *Página 12*, 21 February 2010.

Gil, Sebastián. "Las Islas Malvinas y la Política Exterior Argentina durante los '90s: acerca de su fundamento teórico y de la concepción de una Política de Estado", Serie de Documentos de Trabajo en Internet, Consejo Argentino para las Relaciones Internacionales (CARI), 1999.

González, Martín Abel. "Missed Opportunity? The Anglo-Argentine Negotiations over the Sovereignty of the Falkland Islands, 1966-1968", Documento de Trabajo n° 241, Buenos Aires: Universidad de Belgrano, 2009.

Groussac, Paul. *Las Islas Malvinas*. Buenos Aires: Lugar Editorial, 1982.

Guber, Rosana. *¿Por qué Malvinas? De la causa nacional a la guerra absurda*. Buenos Aires: Fondo de Cultura Económica, 2001.

Guber, Rosana. "¿Qué aprendí?", [online], available at: http://www.unlp.edu.ar/articulo/29/03/2012/especial_malvinas_texto_de_rosana_guber

Guyer, Roberto E. "Cuadrante Austral Sudamericano, entorno internacional, 1989-1999", in Silvia Ruth Jalabé (comp.), *Década de encuentro: Argentina y Gran Bretaña, 1989-1999*. Buenos Aires: CARI, 2001.

Hastings, M. and Jenkins, S. *The Battle for the Falklands*. London: Book Club Associates, 1997.

Hirst, Mónica. "Reflexiones para un análisis político del MERCOSUR", Serie de Documentos e Informes de Investigación del Área de Relaciones Internacionales, n° 120. Buenos Aires: FLACSO, 1991.

Hobsbawm, Eric. *Historia del siglo XX*, Buenos Aires: Grijalbo Mondadori, 2001.

Hoffmann, F. L., and Hoffmann, O. M. *Sovereignty in Dispute: The Falklands/Malvinas, 1493-1982*. Boulder, CO: Westview Press, 1984.

Holmberg, A. M. *¿Cree Ud que los ingleses nos devolverán las Malvinas? Yo no*. Buenos Aires: Editorial Grandes Temas Argentinos, 1977.

Kinney, *National Interest/National Honor: The Diplomacy of the Falklands Crisis*. New York: Praeger, 1989.

Lorenz, Federico. *Las guerras por Malvinas*. Buenos Aires: EDHASA,

2006.

Lorenz, Federico. *Malvinas: Una guerra argentina*. Buenos Aires: Sudamericana, 2009.

Lorenz, Federico. *Unas islas demasiado famosas: Malvinas, historia y política*. Buenos Aires: Capital Intelectual, 2013.

McGuirk, Bernard. "It breaks two to tangle: constructing and deconstructing bridges", in Guillermo Mira and Fernando Pedrosa (eds.), *Revisiting the Falklands-Malvinas Question: Transnational and Interdisciplinary Perspectives*. London: University of London Press, 2021.

McGuirk, Bernard. *Falklands-Malvinas: An Unfinished Business*. London: Splash Editions, 2018.

Merke, Federico. "Las responsabilidades de la política exterior argentina", *Revista Voces en Plan Fénix* n° 4, 2010.

Moreno, J. C. "La visita de Lord Chalfont a Puerto Stanley", in Gambini, H. (ed.), *Crónica documental de las Malvinas*, Vol. I. Buenos Aires: Biblioteca de Redacción, 1982.

Oliveri, Ángel M. *Malvinas: La clave del enigma*. Buenos Aires: Grupo Editor Latinoamericano, 1992.

Ortiz de Rozas, Carlos. *Confidencias diplomáticas*. Buenos Aires: Aguilar, 2011.

Palacios, Alfredo. *Las Islas Malvinas, archipiélago argentino*. Buenos Aires: Comisión nacional de Historia, 1934.

Palermo, Vicente. *Sal en las heridas*. Buenos Aires: Sudamericana, 2007.

Palermo, Vicente. "Malvinas: causa, diplomacia y guerra. Una mirada de la historia a la luz de contribuciones recientes", *Clarín*, 10 June 2006.

Paradiso, José. *Debates y trayectorias de la política exterior argentina*. Buenos Aires: GEL, 1993.

Pastorino, Ana. *El derecho de libre determinación de los pueblos y la población de las islas*. Buenos Aires: EUDEBA, 2013.

Pereyra Ruy, Carlos. "El MERCOSUR y la UNASUR en la actual coyuntura", *Revista Voces en Plan Fénix*, n° 19, 2012.

Petrella, Fernando. "Estudio Preliminar sobre Malvinas", Tomo VIII, CARI, s.f.

Petrella, Fernando. "La disputa de las islas Malvinas y su contexto histórico", available at: www.ancmyp.org.ar/user/files/01%20Malvinas.pdf, 2010.

Petrella, Fernando. "Malvinas, convergencias y disidencias. Condiciones para el reinicio de un dialogo fructífero", in Sánchez, Leandro Enrique and Gomez, Federico Martín (coord.), *Un actor ignorado: La cuestión Malvinas en el Parlamento Nacional*. Buenos Aires:

Prometeo, 2014.

Pevehouse, Jon. "With a Little help from my friends? Regional organizations and the consolidation of democracy", *American Journal of Political Science*, Vol. 46, n° 3, 2002.

Rapoport, Mario. "Argentina: Economía y Política Internacional: Los procesos históricos", in *Diplomacia, Estrategia & Política*, n° 10, 2009.

Rapoport, Mario. *Historia económica, política y social de la Argentina (1880-2003)*. Buenos Aires: Ediciones Macchi, 2007.

Romero, Agustín. *La Política Exterior de Alfonsín y Menem Hacia la Cuestión Malvinas*. Buenos Aires: Ediciones de Belgrano, 1999.

Rozitchner, León. *Las Malvinas: de la guerra sucia a la guerra limpia*. Buenos Aires: Biblioteca de Política Argentina, 1985.

Ruda, José María. "Statement to the Special Committee on the Situation with regard to the Implementation of the Declaration on the Granting of Independence to Colonial Countries and Peoples", 9 September 1964. Available from https://falklandstimeline.files.wordpress.com/2012/02/dr-rudas-speech-to-the-decolonization-committee-1964-annotated.pdf.

Russell, Roberto and Corigliano, Francisco. "El gobierno Menem y las Negociaciones sobre Malvinas", *América Latina Internacional*, vol. 6, n° 22, 1989.

Russell, Roberto and Tokatlian, Juan Gabriel. "De la autonomía antagónica a la autonomía relacional: una mirada teórica desde el cono sur", *Post/Data*, n° 7, 2001.

Russell, Roberto and Tokatlian, Juan Gabriel. *El lugar de Brasil en la política exterior argentina*. Buenos Aires: Fondo de Cultura Económica, 2003.

Russell, Roberto. "Políticas exteriores: hacia una política común", in Rapoport, Mario (ed.), *Argentina y Brasil en el MERCOSUR: Políticas comunes y alianzas regionales*. Buenos Aires: GEL, 1995.

Russell, Roberto. *La Política Exterior Argentina en el Nuevo Orden Mundial*. Buenos Aires: GEL, 1992.

Sabia de Barberis, Gladys. "Análisis de las comisiones creadas a partir de los Acuerdos de Madrid", in Jalabé, Silvia Ruth (comp.), *Década de Encuentro: Argentina y Gran Bretaña 1989-1999*. Buenos Aires: CARI, 2001.

Salmore, Bárbara and Salmore, Stephen. "Political Regimens and Foreign Policy", in Salmore, Stephen, Maurice East and Charles Herman (eds.), *Why Nations Act: Theoretical Perspectives for Comparative Foreign Policy Studies*. Beverly Hills: Sage, 1978.

Shackleton, Edward. *Relevamiento económico de las Islas Malvinas: Informe*, vol. II. Buenos Aires: Instituto Argentino de Estudios Estratégicos y de las Relaciones Internacionales, 1976.

Simonoff, Alejandro. "Los tres modelos históricos de la política exterior argentina", *Jornadas de Relaciones Internacionales Poderes emergentes: ¿Hacia nuevas formas de concertación Internacional?* Buenos Aires: FLACSO, 2010.

Vernet, María Sáez de. *Diario de María Sáez de Vernet en Malvinas.* Buenos Aires: Punto de Encuentro, 2016.

Villareal, Juan. "Los hilos sociales del poder", in Jozami Eduardo (comp.), *Crisis de la dictadura argentina.* Buenos Aires: Siglo XXI, 1985.

Vinuesa, Raúl Emilio. *El conflicto por las Malvinas y el derecho internacional.* Buenos Aires: Centro de Estudios Internacionales, 1985.

Waltz, Kenneth. *Foreign Policy and Democratic Politics.* Boston: Little, Brown and Company, 1967.

Zavala Ortiz, M. A. "Islas Malvinas", *Revista Estrategia*, n° 45, 1977.

Documents

Bilateral Treaties and Understandings between Argentina and the United Kingdom.

"Cuestión de las Islas Malvinas", Ministry of Foreign Affairs and Worship of Argentina, s.f,

Constitución Nacional (Argentina), 1994.

Decree 2.251/2013.

Decree 809/2014.

"Estado de situación de los entendimientos provisorios", Ministry of Foreign Affairs and Worship of Argentina, s.f.

"Estrategia. Relevamiento económico de las Islas Malvinas. Informe Shackleton, vol. II", 1976.

"La Comunidad Internacional y la Cuestión Malvinas", Ministry of Foreign Affairs and Worship of Argentina, s.f.

"Las Naciones Unidas, la Cuestión Malvinas y el principio de libre determinación", March 2013.

Oficio of Bolivia's government, Ministry of Foreign Affairs of Argentina, 1833.

"Posición argentina sobre diversos aspectos de la Cuestión de las Islas Malvinas", Ministry of Foreign Affairs and Worship of Argentina, s/f.

"Posición argentina sobre diversos aspectos de la Cuestión de las Islas

Malvinas", Ministry of Foreign Affairs and Worship of Argentina, s.f.

Presidential inauguration speech, Néstor Kirchner, 25 May 2003.

Presidential inauguration speech, Raúl Alfonsín, 10 December 1983.

Provision 108 of the Undersecretariat of Ports and Inland Waterways.

Rattenbach Report, 1983 (suppressed until 2012).

Resolutions of the Ministry of Energy, n° 128; n° 129; n° 130; n° 131 and n° 133 (2012).

Speech by Ambassador José María Ruda at the United Nations, 1964.

Speech by Marcelo Vernet before the Decolonization Committee, 2012.

Speech by María Angélica Vernet before the Decolonization Committee, 2012.

Speech by Néstor Kirchner, United Nations General Assembly, 2003.

"Tratados Bilaterales Argentina-Reino Unido", Ministry of Foreign Affairs and Worship of Argentina, s.f.

United Nations General Assembly, Resolution 1514 (Xv), 1960. Available from http://undocs.org/A/Res/1514(XV).

United Nations General Assembly, Resolution 2065 (XX), 1965. Available from http://undocs.org/en/a/res/2065(XX).

Vernet, Angélica. Speech to the United Nations Decolonization Committee, 2011.

Vernet, Marcelo. Speech to the United Nations Decolonization Committee, 2012.

Personal interviews

With senior officials

Eduardo Airaldi (10 September 2013): Former ambassador. Director General of Malvinas and South Atlantic of the Ministry of Foreign Affairs of the Nation (2004-2009).

Andrés Cisneros (interview conducted on 3 August 2013): Secretary of Foreign Relations and Latin American Affairs of the Ministry of Foreign Affairs (1996-1999), Secretary General and Coordination (1992-1996), Extraordinary and Plenipotentiary Ambassador. Chief of the Cabinet of the Minister Guido Di Tella (1992-1996), Chief of the Cabinet of the Minister of Defence (1991).

Javier Figueroa (20 September 2013): Ambassador in United Kingdom (2021), Vice-Secretary of Malvinas and South Atlantic of the Ministry of Foreign Affairs (2013-2015), General Director of Malvinas and South Atlantic of the Ministry of Foreign Affairs and Worship (2009-2013).

Fernando Maurette (24 July 2013): Secretary of Military Affairs of the Ministry of Defence (2002-2003), President of the Foreign Relations Commission of the Chamber of Deputies of the Nation (1995-1999).

Fernando Petrella (30 July 2013): Member of the Cabinet of Mr. Chancellor (2004-2007), Undersecretary for Foreign Policy (2002-2003), representative to the Argentine-Spanish Permanent Thought Forum (2001-2002), advisor to the Technical Undersecretary (2000-2001), representative standing before the United Nations, New York (1996-1999), Secretary of State for Foreign Relations and Latin American Affairs (1992-1996), Director General for Politics. Undersecretary for Foreign Policy (1991-1992), Director of the Western Europe Directorate (1990-1991).

Jorge Taiana (26 July 2013): Chancellor (2005-2010), Vice-chancellor (2003-2005), Secretary General of the Inter-American Commission on Human Rights of the Organization of American States (1996-2003).

With islanders and descendants of islanders
Alejandro Betts (September and December 2014).
Guillermo Clifton (September 2014).
Cynthia Dickie (September 2014).
Georgina Gleadell (September 2014).
Michael O'Byrne (September 2014).

Index

The Falklands-Malvinas Conflict

This is a revised and expanded version of the book first published in 2007.

Hors de Combat: The Falklands-Malvinas Conflict in Retrospect brings together contributions from the University of Nottingham's 2006 International Colloquium, The Falklands-Malvinas Conflict Twenty-Five Years On. The initiative to hold such an historic event led to the coming together for the first time since the 1982 War of ex-combatants from both sides, in dialogue with specialist historians, media sociologists, lawyers, literary critics and psychiatrists, as well as with veterans of other wars.

Their contributions, edited by Diego F. García Quiroga and Mike Seear, who themselves served in the War, are published here as a written record of what, for many, had been a unique moment of peace and reconciliation.

210 pp.　ISBN 9781905510252
£6.99 (UK) - $8.99 (US) - €7.99 (EU)
Date of Publication: 1 June 2009

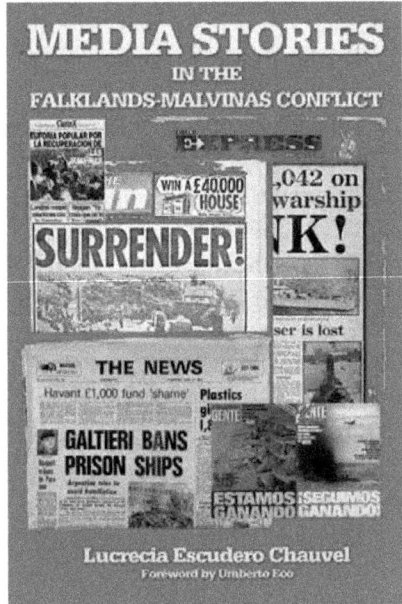

From the Foreword, by Umberto Eco:
"Here is yet another effect of fog, this time provided directly by readers in order to sustain the necessary suspense of the story. We seem to be halfway between Flatland and Antonioni's Blow Up. Argentine newspapers were obliged to find another narrative genre, shifting from war movies to spy novels. Who invented the Yellow Submarine? The British secret services, in order to lower the spirits of Argentines? The Argentine military command, in order to justify its tough stance? The British press? The Argentine press? Who benefited from the rumour? The Yellow Submarine was posited by the media, and as soon as it was posited everyone took it for granted. What happens when in a fictional text the author posits, as an element of the actual world (which is the background of the fictional one) something that does not obtain in the actual world?"

170 pp.　ISBN 9781905510443
£5.99 (UK) - $7.99 (US) - €6.99 (EU)
Date of Publication: 1 October 2014

www.ingramcontent.com/pod-product-compliance
Lightning Source LLC
Chambersburg PA
CBHW071639050426
42443CB00026B/740

Help Yourself Every Day

Thirty Magical Meditations to Help You Manifest Your Best Life Now

Catherine DePino

ARS METAPHYSICA

an imprint of Sunbury Press, Inc.
Mechanicsburg, PA USA

ARS METAPHYSICA

an imprint of Sunbury Press, Inc.
Mechanicsburg, PA USA

For information about special discounts for bulk purchases, please contact Sunbury Press Orders Dept. at (855) 338-8359 or orders@sunburypress.com.

To request one of our authors for speaking engagements or book signings, please contact Sunbury Press Publicity Dept. at publicity@sunburypress.com.

FIRST ARS METAPHYSICA EDITION: June 2020

Set in Adobe Garamond | Interior design by Crystal Devine | Cover design by Terry Kennedy | Edited by Lawrence Knorr.

Publisher's Cataloging-in-Publication Data
Names: DePino, Catherine, author.
Title: Help yourself every day : thirty magical meditations to help you manifest your best life now / Catherine DePino.
Description: First trade paperback edition. | Mechanicsburg, PA : Ars Metaphysica, 2020.
Summary: Author DePino provides many different techniques for spiritual self-improvement.
Identifiers: ISBN: 978-1-620062-64-7 (softcover).
Subjects: BODY, MIND & SPIRIT / Inspiration & Personal Growth | BODY, MIND & SPIRIT / Mindfulness & Meditation | SELF-HELP / Personal Growth / Happiness.

Product of the United States of America
0 1 1 2 3 5 8 13 21 34 55

Continue the Enlightenment!